25-04 BK BUd   12-04   P9-CDM-309

Drug Legalization

Other Books in the Current Controversies Series:

Drug Legalization

Scott Barbour, *Book Editor*

David Bender, *Publisher*
Bruno Leone, *Executive Editor*

Bonnie Szumski, *Editorial Director*
David M. Haugen, *Managing Editor*

CURRENT CONTROVERSIES

Cover photo: © Rommel Pecson/Impact Visuals

Library of Congress Cataloging-in-Publication Data

Drug legalization / Scott Barbour, book editor.
    p. cm. — (Current controversies)
    Includes bibliographical references and index.
    ISBN 0-7377-0336-9 (lib.) — ISBN 0-7377-0335-0 (pbk.)
    1. Drug legalization—United States. 2. Drug abuse—Government
policy—United States. 3. Narcotics, Control of, United States.
I. Barbour, Scott, 1963–   . II. Series.
HV5825 .D77665   2000
364.1'77'0973   99-048084
                                                                         CIP

©2000 by Greenhaven Press, Inc., PO Box 289009, San Diego, CA 92198-9009
Printed in the U.S.A.

Contents

dedicated to working cooperatively with the United States in its effort to
stem the flow of drugs across its borders.

No: Prohibition Is Not an Effective Strategy in the War on Drugs

Chapter 2: Should U.S. Drug Policies Be Liberalized?

Yes: U.S. Drug Policies Should Be Liberalized

No: U.S. Drug Policies Should Not Be Liberalized

Chapter 3: Should Marijuana Laws Be Relaxed?

Yes: Marijuana Laws Should Be Relaxed

No: Marijuana Laws Should Not Be Relaxed

Foreword

By definition, controversies are "discussions of questions in which opposing opinions clash" (Webster's Twentieth Century Dictionary Unabridged). Few would deny that controversies are a pervasive part of the human condition and exist on virtually every level of human enterprise. Controversies transpire between individuals and among groups, within nations and between nations. Controversies supply the grist necessary for progress by providing challenges and challengers to the status quo. They also create atmospheres where strife and warfare can flourish. A world without controversies would be a peaceful world; but it also would be, by and large, static and prosaic.

The Series' Purpose

The purpose of the Current Controversies series is to explore many of the social, political, and economic controversies dominating the national and international scenes today. Titles selected for inclusion in the series are highly focused and specific. For example, from the larger category of criminal justice, Current Controversies deals with specific topics such as police brutality, gun control, white collar crime, and others. The debates in Current Controversies also are presented in a useful, timeless fashion. Articles and book excerpts included in each title are selected if they contribute valuable, long-range ideas to the overall debate. And wherever possible, current information is enhanced with historical documents and other relevant materials. Thus, while individual titles are current in focus, every effort is made to ensure that they will not become quickly outdated. Books in the Current Controversies series will remain important resources for librarians, teachers, and students for many years.

In addition to keeping the titles focused and specific, great care is taken in the editorial format of each book in the series. Book introductions and chapter prefaces are offered to provide background material for readers. Chapters are organized around several key questions that are answered with diverse opinions representing all points on the political spectrum. Materials in each chapter include opinions in which authors clearly disagree as well as alternative opinions in which authors may agree on a broader issue but disagree on the possible solutions. In this way, the content of each volume in Current Controversies mirrors the mosaic of opinions encountered in society. Readers will quickly realize that there are many viable answers to these complex issues. By questioning each author's conclusions, students and casual readers can begin to develop the critical thinking skills so important to evaluating opinionated material.

Current Controversies is also ideal for controlled research. Each anthology in the series is composed of primary sources taken from a wide gamut of informational categories including periodicals, newspapers, books, United States and foreign government documents, and the publications of private and public organizations. Readers will find factual support for reports, debates, and research papers covering all areas of important issues. In addition, an annotated table of contents, an index, a book and periodical bibliography, and a list of organizations to contact are included in each book to expedite further research.

Perhaps more than ever before in history, people are confronted with diverse and contradictory information. During the Persian Gulf War, for example, the public was not only treated to minute-to-minute coverage of the war, it was also inundated with critiques of the coverage and countless analyses of the factors motivating U.S. involvement. Being able to sort through the plethora of opinions accompanying today's major issues, and to draw one's own conclusions, can be a complicated and frustrating struggle. It is the editors' hope that Current Controversies will help readers with this struggle.

Greenhaven Press anthologies primarily consist of previously published material taken from a variety of sources, including periodicals, books, scholarly journals, newspapers, government documents, and position papers from private and public organizations. These original sources are often edited for length and to ensure their accessibility for a young adult audience. The anthology editors also change the original titles of these works in order to clearly present the main thesis of each viewpoint and to explicitly indicate the opinion presented in the viewpoint. These alterations are made in consideration of both the reading and comprehension levels of a young adult audience. Every effort is made to ensure that Greenhaven Press accurately reflects the original intent of the authors included in this anthology.

"All advocates of legalization share the conviction that the current prohibitionist drug policies are not working—that they are in fact making drug-related problems worse—and that liberalization of the nation's drug laws is the only solution."

Introduction

In August 1999, federal agents announced that they had broken up one of America's twenty largest drug rings in a yearlong operation dubbed "Operation Southwest Express." In all, agents indicted 100 suspects, arrested 77, and seized 5,622 pounds of cocaine, 2 tons of marijuana, $1 million in cash, 2 Ferraris, a Land Rover, and 7 weapons. In the process, they disrupted a network of smugglers and dealers that were bringing drugs into the country from Mexico through El Paso and supplying several major cities in the eastern and Midwestern United States, including Chicago, New York, and Boston.

While officials consider drug busts like Operation Southwest Express crucial to America's antidrug efforts, critics of the nation's drug war contend that breaking up one drug ring will have virtually no impact on the availability of drugs. Due to the great demand for illegal drugs in America—and the astronomical profits to be made by supplying them—another drug operation will quickly replace every one dismantled by the federal government. As David D. Boaz, vice president of the Cato Institute, states, "As long as Americans want to use drugs, and are willing to defy the law and pay high prices to do so, drug busts are futile. Other profit-seeking smugglers and dealers will always be ready to step in and take the place of those arrested."

The debate over law-enforcement tactics like Operation Southwest Express reflects the larger debate over drug legalization. Critics of the war on drugs, such as Boaz, contend that drug prohibition is a futile, costly effort that has failed to reduce drug use. They point out that the drug war costs the federal government more than $16 billion a year and that billions more are spent at the state and local levels. As a result of this massive antidrug campaign, four hundred thousand Americans are imprisoned for drug law violations. Sixty percent of federal prisoners and 25 percent of state and local inmates are held on drug charges—mostly for the relatively minor offenses of possession or low-level dealing to fund their personal use.

Despite this enormous effort, drug war opponents argue, drugs remain readily available and their use is increasing. In 1998, the Monitoring the Future Survey conducted by the University of Michigan reported that 90.4 percent of high school seniors say marijuana is "fairly easy" or "very easy" to obtain. The National Household Survey on Drug Abuse (NHSDA), conducted annually by the U.S. Department of Health and Human Services, found that the number of drug users in America has increased from 12 million in 1992 to 13.6 million in 1998. The number of teens reporting drug use within the prior month increased from 5.3 percent in 1992 to 11.4 percent in 1997. Although that number dropped slightly to 9.9 percent in 1998, it still remains well above the 1992 level. Among young adults age eighteen to twenty-four, drug use has risen from 13.3 percent in 1994 to 16.1 percent in 1998. According to opponents of drug prohibition, these numbers are proof that the war on drugs is failing.

Rather than continuing to wage this disastrous war, critics assert, America should legalize drugs. Supporters of legalization contend that easing the nation's drug laws would have numerous benefits. Perhaps most importantly, they say, it would destroy the black market for drugs and the criminality that surrounds it. If drugs were legal and available in the legitimate marketplace, drug smugglers and their networks of dealers would be put out of business. Drug gangs would no longer engage in violent battles for turf. Inner-city children would no longer be lured into drug-dealing gangs. As the American Civil Liberties Union (ACLU) puts it, drug legalization "would sever the connection between drugs and crime that today blights so many lives and communities."

Specific proposals for how to implement legalization vary widely. Libertarians advocate eliminating all federal drug laws. Others call for more modest reforms. Some focus exclusively on legalizing marijuana—either for medical purposes or more general use—while others want laws against all drugs relaxed. Some call for outright legalization, whereas others promote decriminalization—keeping laws on the books but reducing them to misdemeanor offences or enforcing them selectively. Some favor legalizing all drugs but under a system of strict governmental regulation. Despite their differences, all advocates of legalization share the conviction that the current prohibitionist drug policies are not working—that they are in fact making drug-related problems worse—and that liberalization of the nation's drug laws is the only solution.

Opponents of legalization acknowledge that the war on drugs has not succeeded in eliminating drugs from society, but they reject the charge that the effort has been a total failure. While drug use has risen in many categories since the early 1990s, they concede, it is still much lower than it was in the 1970s, prior to the launching of the drug war. In 1979, according to the NHSDA, 14.1 percent of Americans surveyed reported having used an illegal drug during the previous month. That number declined to a low of 5.8 percent in 1992, and although it has since risen to 6.4 percent in 1997, it still remains well below the 1979 level. Drug use among teens shows a similar pattern, dropping from 16.3 percent in 1979 to 5.3 percent in 1992, then rising and falling and eventually hitting 9.9 percent in 1998. Thus, while the drug war has not wiped drugs off the American scene, supporters maintain, it has clearly impacted drug use.

Legalization opponents also reject the argument that liberalizing drug laws would benefit society. They insist that legalizing drugs would inevitably lead to an increase in the use of newly legalized drugs such as marijuana, cocaine, heroin, and amphetamines. As Barry R. McCaffrey, the director of the Office of National Drug Control Policy, states, "Studies show that the more a product is available and legalized, the greater will be its use." This increased drug use would cause a variety of problems, including a decrease in workplace productivity and a rise in automobile and on-the-job accidents, health problems, addiction, and crime. Joseph A. Califano Jr., the president of the National Center on Addiction and Substance Abuse at Columbia University (CASA), explains that although legalization may result in a short-term decrease in drug arrests, the long-term consequences would be devastating: "Any short-term reduction in arrests from repealing drug laws would evaporate quickly as use increased and the criminal conduct—assault, murder, rape, child molestation, and other violence—that drugs like cocaine and methamphetamine spawn exploded."

Opponents of legalization insist that America must continue its antidrug campaign. Some support efforts to reduce the supply of drugs by disrupting international drug cartels and arresting smugglers and dealers. Others favor reducing the demand for drugs through treatment and education. Still others call for a comprehensive approach combining both supply and demand control elements. Despite these differences, all agree that relaxing the drug laws is not the answer to the nation's drug problem. As stated by Charles B. Rangel, a Democratic Congressman from New York, "Rather than holding up the white flag and allowing drugs to take over our country, we must continue to focus on drug demand as well as supply if we are to remain a free and productive society."

The debate over drug legalization, while rooted in real-world concerns over crime, violence, and public health, is also about values. Often a person's position on the issue is based less on the practicality of maintaining or dismantling the nation's drug laws than on underlying beliefs about the morality of drug use. This moral dimension of the drug legalization debate adds another layer of complexity to an already difficult issue. Authors throughout *Drug Legalization: Current Controversies* reflect the full range of opinions on the moral, legal, and public policy aspects of the drug legalization debate as they examine the efficacy of drug prohibition and the advisability of liberalizing the nation's drug laws.

Chapter 1

Is Prohibition an Effective Strategy in the War on Drugs?

Chapter Preface

The U.S. federal government spent nearly $18 billion in its effort to fight drugs in 1999, up from $16 billion in 1998. This money, combined with billions more at the state and local levels, was earmarked for a wide range of programs, including education and prevention, drug treatment, the arrest and conviction of drug dealers and users, and the interdiction of drugs at the nation's borders. This massive antidrug campaign—particularly the law enforcement component of it—is commonly referred to as the "war on drugs."

Critics contend that the war on drugs is a failure and a waste of taxpayers' money. They point out that despite massive spending and aggressive police tactics, drugs remain plentiful on the nation's streets and in the schools. Teen drug use has gone up in recent years, even as spending in the war on drugs has increased. Many critics liken the war on drugs to the prohibition of alcohol in the early twentieth century. That policy resulted in a black market for alcohol and a rise in criminal activity; drug prohibition is having similar results, these critics maintain. Therefore, just as the prohibition of alcohol was eventually repealed, so should drug prohibition be eliminated, or at least relaxed, to eradicate the black market for drugs and the crime and violence associated with the illegal drug trade. As stated by David D. Boaz, vice president of the Cato Institute, "Repeal of prohibition would take the astronomical profits out of the drug business and destroy the kingpins who terrorize U.S. cities."

Others insist that prohibition is a necessary element of the nation's effort to combat drug abuse. Prohibition supporters acknowledge that drug laws have failed to rid society of dangerous drugs, but they insist that ending prohibition would make the problem even worse by lending drugs an aura of respectability and giving young people a green light to abuse harmful substances. Advocates of prohibition disagree over how the war on drugs should be fought; some favor increased drug education, prevention, and treatment programs, while others prefer stronger law enforcement, prosecution of drug dealers and users, and interdiction. However, all agree that drugs themselves—not the prohibition of drugs—are the problem. Barry R. McCaffrey, the director of the White House Office on National Drug Control Policy, sums up the view of those who defend laws against drugs: "Addictive drugs were criminalized because they are harmful; they are not harmful because they were criminalized."

In the following chapter, authors debate the effectiveness of prohibition as a strategy in the nation's battle against drug abuse.

Prohibition Is Essential to the War on Drugs

by John P. Walters and James F.X. O'Gara

About the authors: *John P. Walters is former deputy director of the Office of National Drug Control Policy. James F.X. O'Gara is former drug policy advisor to U.S. senator Orrin Hatch.*

In one of the most compelling TV ads in the White House's new anti-drug campaign, 13-year-old Oakland native Kevin Scott talks about the daily nightmare he faces walking home from school past open-air drug markets. "The dealers are scared of police, but they aren't scared of me. And they don't take 'no' for an answer." The concluding voiceover intones: "To Kevin Scott and all the other kids who take the long way home, we hear you. Don't give up."

Let's hope Kevin and "all the other kids" weren't watching July 9, 1998, when President Clinton essentially told them his latest effort, a $1 billion taxpayer-funded advertising campaign, won't focus on those drug dealers at all. "There are some places where kids are subject to more temptation than others. There are some blocks where there are more drug dealers than others. All of us have to deal with that," said the president, "but we know that the more young people fear drugs, the more they disapprove of them, the less likely they are to use them." Added drug czar Barry McCaffrey, "If you want a war on drugs, you have to sit down at your own kitchen table and talk to your children." Presumably after they've dodged the drug dealers on the way home.

Two days later, in his Saturday radio address, President Clinton had more drug news. But again, he made no mention of the ongoing scandal of open-air drug markets. No, the message for Kevin and "all the other kids" was that the federal government is going to put a few more million tax dollars into the notoriously under-performing drug-treatment system. The Kevins of America might be forgiven for wondering if the adults are really paying attention.

In truth, there is nothing wrong with an ad campaign designed to change youthful attitudes and engage parents and responsible adults. Such campaigns have been effective in the past (when they were funded largely by private contributions)—but only in conjunction with a concerted national effort to target drug use and trafficking on all levels. This time, alas, the ads are being rolled out as a substitute for the national leadership that the president, his drug czar, his Attorney General, and others have failed to supply.

Sen. John Ashcroft astutely said of the new ad campaign: "I do believe that parents need to talk to children,

> *"The attractiveness of drugs can be countered only by moral precepts that are enforced when they are violated."*

but let's do what government is supposed to do and make drug use risky." And where were the rest of our national leaders? Well, Newt Gingrich joined the president at the gala ad-campaign kickoff and proclaimed himself "delighted . . . at what I hope will be a decisive campaign in saving our country and our children from drugs." This is the same Republican leader who has been promising to transform our national anti-drug effort into a real war, "the way we fought World War II."

No serious person can believe that even the best ad campaign is an appropriate centerpiece for the effort to reverse current trends. Consider: Since 1992, drug use by young people has increased more rapidly than at any time since modern measurement began in the 1970s. Never has the age of first use of marijuana, cocaine, heroin, or LSD been lower. Never has the number of emergency-room cases related to drugs been higher—and the data go back more than two decades. Never has the availability of drugs been greater, with record low prices and record high purities. Never have the forces for the wholesale legalization of drug sales and use been more powerful. Never has an administration established a worse record with regard to the drug problem, and never has one been held less accountable.

Enforcement and Punishment Are Needed

Here's the problem: Drug use can be intensely pleasurable, so pleasurable it can lead the user, in all too many cases, to sacrifice everything else for the sake of obtaining and using drugs. The attractiveness of drugs can be countered only by moral precepts that are enforced when they are violated. If those in authority do not address the issue seriously, they teach that drug use is not a serious matter. And if they say drug use is intolerable but fail to act effectively to stop and punish those who sell and use drugs, their actions convey a much more powerful lesson than their words.

Reducing the supply of drugs is critically important because drug use—whether by non-addicts or addicts—is fueled by their very ubiquity. A nation that permits wide availability of dangerous drugs is sending its citizens an unmistakable message: We are largely indifferent to drug use. The wide availability of drugs entails the normalization of drug use. The harsh reality is that drug use begins in experimentation, with a substantial portion of users escalating to addiction, which often ends in death. A free, democratic society ought to display a special intolerance for those things that undermine the capacity of its citizens to be self-governing.

Yet the current trend has been just the reverse—to decriminalize drug use and substitute "harm reduction" for an intolerance of drug trafficking and use. Accept drug use as normal and unavoidable, Americans have been told. The dramatic reductions of the Reagan and Bush years have been attacked as unsustainable largely because they were not sustained. In fairness, one thing the new ads may do is counter some of the drift toward the normalization of drug use (which is why the legalizers have been loudly attacking the campaign).

An Appalling Example of Leniency

To see what's in store if current trends are left unchecked, one need look no farther than Baltimore. Mayor Kurt Schmoke has taken the path of normalization—reducing drug enforcement, distributing clean needles to addicts, and emphasizing treatment and "harm reduction." For all this, the legalization movement has celebrated Schmoke as a national hero. Baltimore has not only gotten its full measure of federal drug-control funds, it has even received special, additional federal money, as well as $25 million for "harm reduction" efforts from the drug-legalizing philanthropist George Soros.

> *"Responsible adults need to teach young people that drug use is wrong . . . and that . . . those who sell and use drugs will be punished."*

Yet President Clinton's own drug-policy office recently published a stark description of the appalling conditions in Baltimore: Heroin is readily available, with city dealers moving into suburbs and high schools; cocaine is plentiful in both crack and powder forms; and marijuana, a law-enforcement official reports, "is not being seen as a drug." In fact, since Schmoke took office in 1987, Baltimore has become the most addiction-ridden metropolitan area in the country per capita. Washington, D.C., had 89 emergency-room cases related to cocaine per 100,000 in population in 1996—Baltimore had 362. Washington had 40 such cases related to heroin per 100,000 population in 1996—Baltimore had 346. Welcome to the brave new world.

Leaders Must Act Responsibly

Parents and responsible adults need to teach young people that drug use is wrong and harmful and that for this reason those who sell and use drugs will be punished. Television ads may be of some help, but what is vital is that national leaders at the same time carry out their responsibilities: in foreign policy, holding source and transit countries accountable for stopping the flow; in defense policy, making interdiction a priority; and in law enforcement, insisting that major trafficking organizations are systematically targeted and dismantled by federal authorities and that open-air drug markets are closed by local authorities. Treatment that works (including faith-based treatment programs) should be funded.

Americans will take care of what happens around the kitchen table if our leaders will only pay more attention to what happens in the streets. Think about that the next time you see Kevin Scott on television.

Drug Prohibition Is Effective

by Donnie Marshall

About the author: *Donnie Marshall is the deputy administrator of the Drug Enforcement Administration (DEA), the arm of the U.S. Department of Justice that is responsible for enforcing the nation's drug laws.*

Editor's note: The following viewpoint is excerpted from testimony delivered before the U.S. House of Representatives Subcommittee on Criminal Justice, Drug Policy, and Human Resources, Committee on Government Reform, June 16, 1999.

I would like to discuss what I believe would happen if drugs were legalized. I realize that much of the current debate has been over the legalization of so-called medical marijuana. But I suspect that medical marijuana is merely the first tactical maneuver in an overall strategy that will lead to the eventual legalization of all drugs.

Whether all drugs are eventually legalized or not, the practical outcome of legalizing even one, like marijuana, is to increase the amount of usage among all drugs. It's been said that you can't put the genie back in the bottle or the toothpaste back in the tube. I think those are apt metaphors for what will happen if America goes down the path of legalization. Once America gives into a drug culture, and all the social decay that comes with such a culture, it would be very hard to restore a decent civic culture without a cost to America's civil liberties that would be prohibitively high. . . .

Drug Enforcement Works

This is no time to undermine America's effort to stem drug abuse. America's drug policies work. From 1979 to 1994, the number of drug users in America dropped by almost half. Two things significantly contributed to that outcome. First, a strong program of public education; second, a strict program of law enforcement.

Excerpted from testimony given by Donnie Marshall before the U.S. House of Representatives, Government Reform and Oversight Committee, Subcommittee on Criminal Justice, Drug Policy, and Human Resources, June 16, 1999, Washington, D.C.

If you look over the last four decades, you can see a pattern develop. An independent researcher, R. E. Peterson, has analyzed this period, using statistics from a wide variety of sources, including the Justice Department and the White House Office of National Drug Control Strategy. He broke these four decades down into two periods: the first, from 1960 to 1980, an era of permissive drug laws; the second, from 1980 to 1995, an era of tough drug laws.

During the permissive period, drug incarceration rates fell almost 80 percent. During the era of tough drug laws, drug incarceration rates rose almost 450 percent. Just as you might expect, these two policies regarding drug abuse had far different consequences. During the permissive period, drug use among teens climbed by more than 500 percent. During the tough era, drug use by high school students dropped by more than a third.

Is there an absolute one-to-one correlation between tougher drug enforcement and a declining rate of drug use? I wouldn't suggest that. But the contrasts of drug abuse rates between the two eras of drug enforcement are striking.

Drug Abuse Is Not Inevitable

One historian of the drug movement has written about America's experience with the veterans of Vietnam. As you may recall from the early 1970s, there was a profound concern in the American government over the rates of heroin use by our military personnel in Vietnam. At the time, U.S. Army medical officers estimated that about 10–15 percent of the lower ranking enlisted men in Vietnam were heroin users.

Military authorities decided to take a tough stand on the problem. They mandated a drug test for every departing soldier. Those who failed were required to undergo drug treatment for 30 days. The theory was that many of the soldiers who were using heroin would give it up to avoid the added 30 days in Vietnam. It clearly worked. Six months after the tests began, the percentage of soldiers testing positive dropped from 10 percent to two percent.

There may be a whole host of reasons for this outcome. But it demonstrates that there is nothing inevitable about drug abuse. In fact, the history of America's experience with drugs has shown us that it was strong drug enforcement that effectively ended America's first drug epidemic, which lasted from the mid-1880s to the mid-1920s.

> *"It was strong drug enforcement that effectively ended America's first drug epidemic, . . . from the mid-1880s to the mid-1920s."*

By 1923, about half of all prisoners at the Federal penitentiary in Leavenworth, Kansas, were violators of America's first drug legislation, the Harrison Act. If you are concerned by the high drug incarceration rates of the late 1990s, consider the parallels to the tough drug enforcement policies of the 1920s. It was those tough policies that did much to create America's virtually drug-free environment of the mid-20th century.

Drug laws can work, if we have the national resolve to enforce them. As a father, as someone who's had a lot of involvement with the Boy Scouts and Little Leaguers, and as a 30-year civil servant in drug enforcement, I can tell you that there are a lot of young people out there looking for help. Sometimes helping them means saying "no," and having the courage to back it up.

An Effective Arrest

Let me tell you a story about one of them. He was a young man who lived near Austin, Texas. He had a wife who was pregnant. To protect their identities, I'll call them John and Michelle. John was involved in drugs, and one night we arrested him and some of his friends on drug charges. He went on to serve a six-month sentence before being turned loose.

> *"America's experience with drugs shows that strong law enforcement policies can and do work."*

Sometime after he got out, he and his wife came to our office looking for me. They rang the doorbell out at the reception area, and my secretary came back and said they were here to see me. I had no idea what they wanted. I was kind of leery, thinking they might be looking for revenge. But I went out to the reception area anyway.

John and Michelle were standing there with a little toddler. They said they just wanted to come in so we could see their new baby. And then Michelle said there was a second reason they came by. When he got arrested, she said, that's the best thing that ever happened to them.

We had been very wholesome people, she said. John was involved in sports in high school. He was an all-American guy. Then he started smoking pot. His parents couldn't reach him. His teachers couldn't reach him. He got into other drugs. He dropped out of high school. The only thing that ever got his attention, she said, was when he got arrested.

Meanwhile, John was listening to all this and shaking his head in agreement. He said that his high school coach had tried to counsel him, but he wouldn't listen to him. He said his big mistake was dropping out of sports. He thought that if he had stayed in sports he wouldn't have taken the route he did.

When I arrested those kids that night I had no idea of the extent to which I would ultimately help them out of their problems and influence their lives in a positive way. In 30 years of dealing with young Americans, I believe that John is more typical than not.

America spends millions of dollars every year on researching the issue of drugs. We have crime statistics and opinion surveys and biochemical research. And all of that is important. But what it all comes down to is whether we can help young people like John—whether we can keep them from taking that first step into the world of drugs that will ruin their careers, destroy their marriages and leave them in a cycle of dependency on chemicals.

Whether in rural areas, in the suburbs, or in the inner cities, there are a lot of kids who could use a little help. Sometimes that help can take the form of education and counseling. Often it takes a stronger approach. And there are plenty of young people, and older people as well, who could use it.

If we as a society are unwilling to have the courage to say no to drug abuse, we will find that drugs will not only destroy the society we have built up over 200 years, but ruin millions of young people like John.

Drug abuse, and the crime and personal dissolution and social decay that go with it, are not inevitable. Too many people in America seem resigned to the growing rates of drug use. But America's experience with drugs shows that strong law enforcement policies can and do work.

At DEA, our mission is to fight drug trafficking in order to make drug abuse the most expensive, unpleasant, risky, and disreputable form of recreation a person could have. If drug users aren't worried about their health, or the health and welfare of those who depend on them, they should at least worry about the likelihood of getting caught. Not only do tough drug enforcement policies work, but I might add that having no government policy, as many are suggesting today, is in fact a policy, one that will reap a whirlwind of crime and social decay.

The War on Drugs Should Focus on Reducing the Drug Supply

by Bill McCollum

About the author: *Bill McCollum is a Republican senator from Florida.*

No discussion on the merits of drug legalization is legitimate unless it is prefaced by these alarming, undisputed facts:
- Teen drug use has doubled since 1992;
- Nearly half of all 17-year-olds say they could buy marijuana within an hour;
- The number of heroin-related emergency-room admissions jumped 58 percent between 1992 and 1995;
- And, most shockingly, illegal drugs and drug-related crime and violence kill 20,000 Americans a year, at a cost of $67 billion.

If thousands of young Americans were killed in Bosnia or in any other place across the globe, there would be riots in the streets.

And yet, even with these troubling statistics as a backdrop, a small, vocal minority are advocating drug legalization as the cure for our nation's drug crisis. I can't think of a more grim proposal for our children and our nation.

Legalization's Effects

Many legalization advocates argue that if drugs were legalized, crime and violence would decrease. The commonsense response to that argument is that the already unacceptably high level of teen drug use undoubtedly would soar even higher, dragging in its wake the societal problems that accompany drug use. The reality is that drug use is almost always a contributing factor to criminal behavior.

According to a survey of state prison inmates, 28 percent of prisoners convicted of murder, 20 percent of inmates convicted of sexual assault and 23 percent of inmates convicted of assault were under the influence of drugs when they committed their crimes. Another study indicated that drug users were 10 times more likely to commit a violent act than nondrug users. Drug use and crime go hand in hand—it is that simple. In fact, history has demonstrated the reverse effect drug legalization would have on crime rates. When California attempted to decriminalize marijuana in 1976, arrests for driving under the influence of drugs rose 46 percent among adults and 71.4 percent among juveniles within the first six months.

> *"America has not been waging a true war on drugs."*

Another myth often associated with the legalization movement is that revenue and taxes from the sale of drugs would help boost the economy. This claim is flawed at best and unsubstantiated by facts. The economic benefit, if any, would be eclipsed by the billions spent treating the societal ills caused by drug abuse. The Drug Enforcement Administration, or DEA, estimates drug legalization would cost society between $140 billion and $210 billion a year in lost productivity and job-related accidents.

For instance, total tax revenue from the sale of alcohol is $13.1 billion a year, but alcohol extracts more than $100 billion a year in social costs such as health care and lost productivity. There is no evidence that taxing narcotics such as cocaine, heroin and marijuana would bolster revenues any more than alcohol does. And the expected revenue certainly would not offset the social and medical costs.

Legalization Masquerading as Compassion

With 90 percent of the public against drug legalization, proponents have masked their tactics with phrases such as "drug reform," "medicalization" and "harm reduction." In an effort to chip away at our nation's drug laws, groups are promoting the adoption of loosely worded state ballot initiatives that would legalize marijuana for "medicinal use."

With clear evidence of marijuana's gateway effect—12- to 17-year-olds who use marijuana are 85 times more likely to use cocaine than those who abstain—these efforts are quite troubling. The cavalier labeling of a dangerous and highly addictive drug as "medicine" sends the wrong message to our youth.

An initiative that was proposed for the fall 1998 ballot in Washington, D.C.—where 96 percent of all youth arrested for crime test positive for marijuana—would permit individuals to legally use marijuana for medical treatment when recommended by a licensed physician. No written prescription would be required. Like its highly publicized predecessors in California and Arizona, this initiative would have made growing, trafficking and possessing marijuana legal for almost any ailment. Unlike all other drugs used to treat illness or pain, no Food and Drug Administration, or FDA, approval would be necessary. When almost anyone could find a physician to recommend smoking marijuana for any ailment, policing illegal use and trafficking would become a practical impossibility.

While I do not possess the medical or scientific expertise to pass judgment on whether marijuana is a medicine, the FDA does. So do the National Institutes of Health, the American Medical Association, the American Cancer Society and the National Multiple Sclerosis Association. Yet, each and every one of these esteemed organizations has concluded marijuana has no medicinal value. The collective expert judgment of these organizations and the long-established FDA drug approval process cannot be ignored simply because some people want to label marijuana "medicine." Science cannot be based on opinion polls.

For three decades, marijuana has been classified as a Schedule I drug, meaning it has a high potential for abuse, lacks any currently accepted medical use and is unsafe, even under medical supervision. According to the National Institute of Allergy and Infectious Diseases, HIV-positive smokers of marijuana progress to full-blown AIDS twice as fast as nonsmokers and have an increased incidence of bacterial pneumonia.

There is no doubt that these campaigns are more about drug legalization than about providing relief for the sick and dying. In 1993, Richard Cowen, director of the National Organization for the Reform of Marijuana Laws, declared ". . . medical marijuana is our strongest suit. It is our point of leverage which will move us toward the legalization of marijuana for personal use, and in that process we will begin to break down the power of the narcocracy to wage a war of terror over things."

I can think of no political strategy more unseemly than drug legalization masquerading as compassion. Voters and, more importantly, the seriously ill, deserve the facts, not emotional half-truths.

Interdiction Efforts Must Be Increased

Legalization advocates point out that despite ongoing efforts, drug use is up. So why not wave the white flag in the drug war? While it's true that drugs are cheaper and more plentiful than ever before on the streets of America, now is not the time to abandon our efforts. The truth is, America has not been waging a true war on drugs. The lack of a balanced anti-narcotics strategy has played a key role in the rise in drug use. Not a single U.S. military airplane or warship is assigned to interdiction efforts in the Eastern Pacific between Colombia, Mexico and the United States. The number of flight and steaming hours spent patrolling the Caribbean Sea and Gulf of Mexico has been cut by two-thirds since 1992. With the exception of the U.S.-Mexico border effort, resources to intercept drugs entering the country from source countries and the transit zone have also been cut by two-thirds since 1992.

"Reducing the flow of drugs entering the United States must be a top priority."

Despite clear evidence that a balanced approach to the drug war achieved real success (from 1988 to 1991, cocaine use dropped by 35 percent and marijuana use dropped by 16 percent), in mid-1993 the Clinton administration made a very public, "controlled shift" in its drug strategy. This shift resulted in increased funding for prevention and treatment efforts at the expense of interdiction efforts. Since 1993, funds dedicated to international interdiction efforts have continued to languish around 13 percent of total federal expenditures on the drug war, as opposed to the 33 percent allotted in 1987.

"Prevent drugs from entering the country and you drive up the price of drugs. Drive up the price of drugs and you save lives."

The result? Quantity is up, price is down and more kids are becoming users. Let's not kid ourselves. Drug trafficking is a business. The less it costs to grow and transport illegal drugs into this country, the lower the price of drugs on the street. Therefore, reducing the flow of drugs entering the United States must be a top priority. Until the availability of drugs is dramatically reduced and the price driven up, education and law-enforcement efforts cannot be expected to succeed in any meaningful way.

The Benefits of Cooperation

All the cocaine entering the United States originates in Colombia, Peru and Bolivia. Most of the heroin in the country is grown and produced in Colombia. When I visited these countries in 1998, key U.S. antinarcotics personnel told me that the supply of drugs leaving those countries could be reduced by 80 percent in only a couple of years if our government would commit the necessary resources and adjust its policies in cooperation with the source-country governments.

Peru, which already has adopted more aggressive tactics, is producing results. In the two years since Peruvian President Alberto Fujimori implemented a get-tough, antitrafficking and crop-eradication program—including shooting down drug smugglers' aircraft—cocaine production in Peru has dropped 40 percent. With more U.S. support, victory over the narcotics trade in Peru is within reach. The same could be accomplished in Bolivia and Colombia with the cooperation of their governments and a continued U.S. effort to keep radar and tracking planes in the air 24 hours a day.

A True War Is Needed

A continued investment in demand-reduction strategies is critical. I strongly support finding ways to persuade Americans that doing drugs is wrong—that it destroys lives, families, schools and communities. But we need a comprehensive counter-drug strategy that addresses all components of this problem. The lesson of the past decade is simple: Prevent drugs from entering the country and you drive up the price of drugs. Drive up the price of drugs and you save lives.

Unfortunately, a lot has changed in recent years. Instead of a comprehensive drug-education effort in our schools, homes and workplaces, we see attitudes of indifference and ambivalence. The legalization movement is but one reason why the message that drug use is both destructive and wrong has been lost. Sadly, today's youth increasingly see no harm in using drugs.

This dramatic reversal in trends spells grave harm for both the present and the future. We owe it to our kids to wage a true war on drugs.

An International Drug Prohibition Effort Is Needed

by Barry R. McCaffrey

About the author: *Barry R. McCaffrey is director of the Office of National Drug Control Policy, a position commonly referred to as "drug czar."*

Though no single issue dominates our Hemispheric agenda, the overall problem of illegal drugs and related crimes represents a direct threat to the health and well-being of the peoples of the [Western] Hemisphere. All of us here today recognize that we cannot afford to let the demand for and cultivation, production, distribution, trafficking, and sale of illicit narcotics and psychotropic substances interfere with the aspirations of our peoples. Illegal drugs inflict staggering costs on our societies. They kill and sicken our people, sap productivity, drain economies, threaten the environment, and undermine democratic institutions and international order. Drugs are a direct attack on our children and grandchildren. If we are to make inroads against this growing problem, we shall only do so collectively. We can make progress by formulating a common understanding of the problems posed by drug production, trafficking, and consumption and by developing cooperative approaches and solutions. That's exactly the vision spelled out in the Inter-American Drug Abuse Control Commission (CICAD) Hemispheric Anti-Drug Strategy. If we act on it, we can prevent illegal drugs from darkening the promising dawn of the new millennium.

The Consequences of Drug Abuse in the United States

The consequences of illegal drug use have been devastating within the United States. We estimate that in the 1990s alone, drug use has cost our society more than 100,000 dead and some $300 billion. Each year, more than 500,000 Americans must go to hospital emergency rooms because of drug-induced problems. Our children view drugs as the most important problem they face. Drugs and

Excerpted from a speech given by Barry R. McCaffrey to the Twenty-First Regular Session of the Inter-American Drug Abuse Control Commission of the Organization of American States, April 9, 1997, Washington, D.C.

crime are a problem for all Americans, not just city residents, the poor, or minorities. Americans from every social and economic background, race, and ethnic group are concerned about the interrelated problems of crime, violence, and drugs. We fear the violence that surrounds drug markets. We abhor the effect it has on our children's lives. Americans are especially concerned about the increased use of drugs by young people. Today, dangerous drugs like cocaine, heroin, and meth-

> *"If we are to make inroads against this growing problem, we shall only do so collectively."*

amphetamines are cheaper and more potent than they were at the height of our domestic drug problem fifteen or twenty years ago. In Arizona, ninety percent of homicides in 1996 were related to methamphetamines. No nation can afford such devastating social, health, and criminal consequences.

Demand: The Root Cause of the Drug Problem

No one should doubt that the demand for illegal drugs lies at the heart of the global drug problem. We in the United States are cognizant that we are a big part of the demand side of the drug equation. However, the percentage of our citizens that consumes drugs is not the central problem. Currently about six percent of our population, or twelve million Americans use drugs, a reduction of fifty percent from 1979's twenty five million. Even the number of casual cocaine users is down seventy-five percent over the past decade. There are probably 600,000 heroin addicts in the United States. They represent but a fraction of the world's opium/heroin addicts and consume less than two percent of the global heroin production capacity. A total of about 3.6 million Americans, or less than two percent of our population are addicted to illegal drugs. This drug usage causes fourteen thousand deaths and costs $67 billion each year.

The problem is that American drug users have enormous quantities of disposable income. A crack addict in New York can either afford a three hundred and fifty dollar a week habit or steal with relative ease three thousand or more dollars worth of property to maintain that habit. Indeed Americans spend about fifty billion dollars a year on illegal drugs. The wholesale value of cocaine, for example, at U.S. ports of entry of the estimated three hundred metric tons of cocaine that are smuggled into the United States every year is ten billion dollars. The retail value of that cocaine on our streets is thirty billion dollars. These enormous sums are the reason criminal organizations dominate the international traffic in illegal drugs, threaten our communities, and attack our institutions. All of us should recognize that the traffickers of cocaine, heroin, and the other drugs of abuse are actively seeking to develop new markets. If any one of us successfully reduces our consumption of these drugs yet they remain available, they will find new markets. Those new markets, and the addicts and devastation that accompany them, will increasingly be in those countries that produce the drugs and those through which they transit.

The U.S. *National Drug Control Policy* recognizes this reality and prioritizes our efforts accordingly. Our number one goal is to prevent the sixty-eight million Americans under eighteen from becoming a new generation of addicts. We find it unacceptable that drug use rates have doubled among our youth since 1992; we must and will reverse this trend. While we know that we can't arrest our way out of the drug problem, we will also continue to uphold our severe drug laws. A million and a half Americans are now behind bars, many for drug law violations. More than a million more Americans are arrested every year for drug offenses. Incarceration is entirely appropriate for many drug-related crimes. There must be strong incentives to stay clear of drug trafficking, and prison sentences can motivate people to obey the law. Our challenge is to address the problem of chronic drug use by bringing drug testing, assessment, referral, treatment, and supervision within the oversight of the U.S. criminal justice system. We are doing so by increasing the number of drug courts that oversee treatment and rehabilitation for drug law violators and by validating the Office of National Drug Control Policy's (ONDCP) "Break the Cycle" concept. As a nation, we are optimistic that we can substantially reduce the demand for illegal drugs in the United States. One initiative which we believe will help us in this effort is the $175 million-a-year anti-drug campaign . . . launched in the 1998 fiscal year.

A Shared Problem

We recognize that domestic efforts by themselves cannot address what is fundamentally a global problem fueled by powerful, international criminal organizations. All our countries are affected by the drug problem but not necessarily in the same ways. For some, the most pressing issue is drug consumption. For others, it may be drug-related violence and corruption. Some countries are affected by illicit production or trafficking. Other countries are beset by all these problems. No country is immune.

Over the past years, countries in the Western Hemisphere have made strong efforts to curtail production of illicit drugs, their trafficking, and the laundering of drug moneys. Peru's bilateral and multilateral counterdrug cooperation has been notable. President Alberto Fujimori is committed to eliminating coca destined for illicit drug production. The joint U.S.-Peruvian air interdiction campaign forced down, seized and/or destroyed 23 narcotics aircraft in 1995. As a result, narcotics-related flights decreased by 47 percent compared to 1994. This campaign caused coca base prices to fall to record low levels in 1996, providing a critical economic disincentive for campesino grow-

> *"There must be strong incentives to stay clear of drug trafficking, and prison sentences can motivate people to obey the law."*

ers. We believe it was an important contributing factor to the Peruvian Government's success in reducing coca cultivation by eighteen percent in 1996. Brazil has drafted key money laundering legislation and passed comprehensive legislation on regulation of precursor chemicals. The Government of Panama has been a key supporting player in an increasingly sophisticated and effective regional effort to disrupt drug trafficking patterns within South America and of international anti-money laundering initiatives. Our interdiction efforts in the so-called "transit zone" have been enhanced by the eighteen bilateral cooperative agreements we have with a number of Caribbean states. And in Colombia, Attorney General Alfonso Valdivieso, Foreign Minister Emma Maria Mejia, Minister of Defense Gilberto Echeverry, Armed Forces Commander General Harold Bedoya, and National Police Director General Rosso Jose Serrano continue to vigorously oppose narcoguerrillas who are attacking the very institutions of democracy.

> *"The world community cannot allow international criminal organizations to gain a foothold in any country."*

U.S.-Mexican Counterdrug Cooperation

By any measure, the U.S. and Mexico have made significant progress in our joint efforts to face up to the drug problem. Whether we speak of investigations of drug trafficking organizations, anti-smuggling projects, crop eradication efforts, demand reduction programs, or anti-crime legislation, our record of cooperation is substantial.

President Ernesto Zedillo has an obvious commitment to political, legal and institutional reform, and is dedicated to fighting drug trafficking which he has identified as the principal threat to Mexico's national security. Under his leadership, Mexican drug seizures have increased notably, with marijuana seizures up 40% over 1994 and opium-related seizures up 41%. Cocaine, methamphetamine and precursor chemical seizures also rose significantly. No other nation in the world has eradicated as many hectares of illegal drugs as has Mexico. Our extensive bilateral counterdrug cooperation occurs under the rubric of the US/Mexico High Level Contact Group for Drug Control. This bilateral drug control policy group was established in March 1996 and has enabled us to advance our collective effort to thwart drug trafficking and the demand for drugs in both nations.

Our two great nations share many common drug problems. But we have resolved to address them forthrightly, while affirming our commitment to respecting the principles of international law, particularly those of national sovereignty, territorial integrity and nonintervention in the internal affairs of other countries. . . .

More International Cooperation Is Needed

As President Bill Clinton's March 1997 report to Congress on the status of International Drug Trafficking and Abuse suggests, international cooperation requires further strengthening. Illicit poppy cultivation for opium increased 11 percent globally from 1994 to 1995, doubling in one country since 1992. Ominously for the U.S., our Drug Enforcement Agency estimates that Colombia was the source of 60 percent of the heroin seized in the United States in 1996. Ten years ago, there was no opium growing in Colombia. Many valiant Colombians have since died fighting this terrible drug trade. Many source country governments face major threats to their democratic institutions from the destructive effects of drug violence and corruption. Finally, all of us face the terrible threat of the billions of dollars of illegal funds that seriously distort our economic development and threaten the very integrity of our banking systems.

The time has come for all of us as responsible governments to understand that the world community cannot allow international criminal organizations to gain a foothold in any country. The April 1996 meeting in Vienna of the UN Commission on Narcotic Drugs and the Economic and Social Council (ECOSOC) Conference at the UN Headquarters in New York in June 1996 underscored the international consensus for cooperation that will: limit money laundering; control precursor chemicals; take action against institutions or companies facilitating the drug trade; develop procedures for boarding vessels suspected of carrying illegal drugs; and reduce demand for these substances.

The United States Government is absolutely committed to helping all nations achieve full compliance with the goals and objectives set forth by the United Nations in its 1988 Convention. We will support regional and sub-regional efforts to address drug production, trafficking, and consumption. We will share information with our partners. We are prepared to assist in institution-building so that judiciaries, legislatures, and law enforcement agencies successfully can counter international traffickers. We will support an international effort to stop money laundering. The magnitude of drug profits that filter through international financial institutions makes them conspicuous. Such sums are difficult to conceal from attentive bankers and governments working together. The U.S. government will continue working with our hemispheric partners to develop means of identifying and seizing illegal drug proceeds as they pass through banking systems.

> *"Collective cooperative action holds the promise of reducing trafficking."*

We Must All Redouble Our Commitment

The drug problem is a shared agony throughout this Hemisphere. It affects us all differently. In the United States, drug abuse has enormous health consequences and also generates violent crime and unsafe streets. In Mexico, the problem is different. Geography and a common two-thousand mile border have drawn international drug trafficking organizations to that country as a route to the United States. In the Caribbean, small island nations find it difficult to pro-

tect their extensive coast lines with constrained resources. Collective cooperative action holds the promise of reducing trafficking through this transit zone.
In Colombia and Peru, drug cultivation and production now provides resources
to narcoguerrilla organizations. While the drug abuse menace is a common
problem for all of us, it takes on different forms. All of us must guard against
allowing drug trafficking organizations from gaining a strangle hold on our
economies, our families or our democratic processes.

Mexico Is Committed to Cooperation with U.S. Drug Prohibition Efforts

by Gustavo Gonzalez-Baez

About the author: *Gustavo Gonzalez-Baez is political affairs adviser to the Embassy of Mexico in Washington, D.C.*

The production, trafficking, and consumption of illegal drugs is one of the most serious problems faced by humankind today, both in terms of the damage done to our societies and the breakdown of government institutions. This disastrous double outcome represents a serious public-health challenge, and a threat to national security.

Both government and society are the victims of this terrible and corrupting scourge that kills and destroys. Transnational organized crime stops at nothing to control all the elements of this deadly business—from the harvesting of the drug in Asia and Latin America, to its retail sale in cities and schools in the consuming countries and the inevitable money laundering of drug profits.

The international community has slowly come to the view that this is a worldwide problem, and that to combat it requires global strategies with the participation and shared responsibility of all countries, without distinctions of hemispheres.

However, the task of reaching regional and multilateral consensus and agreements has not been an easy one. Precious time is lost due to mistrust and the inability to quickly reach accords at international forums. This slowness to react works against us, since criminal activity moves at a rapid pace within our countries, using consumption to weaken government structures. Moreover, organized crime is amazingly effective at applying the latest technology in weapons and communications equipment to its own ends, while in poor countries—who cannot respond in a like manner—drug trafficking proliferates with impunity.

An Affront to Modern States

In combating organized crime, it is not sufficient for a country to be democratically and economically strong because organized crime has no trouble finding—or buying—protection and accomplices within the bureaucracy, police corps and the business sector. Consequently, each government must organize its law-enforcement capabilities against crime based on sound legislation as the essential legal element for effective prosecution. And it is necessary to have honest, well-paid, and properly trained police forces and prosecutors, for they are the implementing arm of justice.

But that is not all. The final objective of a well-guided justice system is to imprison drug traffickers with long sentences and seize their assets. All these elements provide the basic framework of a criminal justice system working in the right direction.

However distressing the existence of organized crime is to the international community, there are no magic solutions to eradicate it. Each country must define its national strategy based on its own priorities and the principles it has decided to observe in conjunction with other nations. A country's drug-combating program must be defined within its borders and not imposed from abroad. Any nation's attempt at meddling in another nation's affairs is bound to result in isolation and/or confrontation. The same goes for the practice of certifying a country's performance in combating drug traffic, particularly when the nation passing judgment has not herself been successful in any of the various drug fronts.

Mexico's Effort

The overcoming of the illegal-drug problem—and the wake of crime and insecurity it leaves behind—is a complex and arduous task ripe with successes and setbacks. In Mexico, government and society are determined to work to the extent of their ability and talent in combating crime and impunity in drug trafficking. However, the huge wealth of the drug traffickers undermines and corrupts our police forces and Mexican prosecutors are not always sufficiently trained to conduct the necessary investigations. The Mexican judicial branch does not always act as it should to send these criminals behind bars for a long period of time.

> *"In Mexico, government and society are determined to work to the extent of their ability and talent in combating crime and impunity in drug trafficking."*

And yet, Mexico has made great strides, which have received international recognition:

No country in the world eradicates a greater number of illegal-drug fields than Mexico. Thirty thousand hectares are destroyed annually, with the help of 20,000 Mexican soldiers.

The measures taken by Mexico to combat money laundering are too showing results in record time.

A new Mexican federal law for combating organized crime introduces forms of criminal investigation that were unknown in Mexico only two years ago and provides more tools for dismantling the major drug-trafficking cartels. Mexico's most recent successes in this area include the arrest of an entire drug-trafficking band, the dismantling of three criminal organizations involved in kidnapping, and also the dismantling of the Amezcua Contreras brothers' cartel.

> *"Mexico's interception efforts on its southern border are proof of its earnest desire to stop the flow of drugs from South American countries to the U.S. market."*

Mexico's interception efforts on its southern border are proof of its earnest desire to stop the flow of drugs from South American countries to the U.S. market.

Programs are being implemented to replace federal law-enforcement personnel through the use of several background checks and screening methods, including lie-detector tests. Measures have also been taken at the Police Training Institute to prepare police forces to withstand any attempts at corruption.

Cooperation with the United States

Mexico and the United States share an over two-thousand mile border. A total of 254 million persons, 75 million cars, and 3 million freight trucks cross the border annually, through 39 entry points—which represents impressive transborder activity. This provides many opportunities for legitimate trade between the two countries, but it also means that, year after year, large volumes of drugs are smuggled into the United States in response to the great demand for drugs.

There have been problems in terms of our respective political approaches to combating illegal drugs and drug-related crime. Strategies that mistakenly placed greater emphasis on reducing the supply of drugs, and prejudiced attitudes seeking to blame others for the U.S. drug problem, led to confrontation between the two countries. Meanwhile, organized crime gained ground on the streets and in our schools and households, both in Mexico and the United States.

For many years we have engaged in mutual recriminations, and our timid attempts at cooperation have been lost in an atmosphere of mistrust and suspicion. And such attitudes have not completely disappeared, spurred on by the mass media.

A Mechanism for Cooperation

Fortunately, when all sensible arguments for coordinating forces seemed to be ignored, our countries were able to create a mechanism for binational cooperation and action between the two governments. This led to a joint threat assessment, followed by an alliance and a binational strategy that provides balance and structure to our commitments on the basis of the principles of respect to the national sovereignty of each nation.

A High Level Contact Group was created in March of 1996, pursuant to a specific mandate by presidents Ernesto Zedillo and Bill Clinton. The group provides an official framework and has led to greater mutual respect and a more structured and consistent effort on the part of both countries to comply with the commitments made in the binational strategy against drugs. The strategy covers all aspects of the drug problem, through expert groups on: demand reduction, drug interception, money laundering, drug eradication, interdiction, chemical precursors and firearms trafficking.

In order for this bilateral effort to be lasting and have positive results, we must work within the framework of the strategy and review our progress and setbacks with a critical but respectful attitude. We must make whatever changes are necessary and continue fighting without respite to preserve the health of our young people and our societies as a whole. There is no room for complacency and misplaced pride in this social and political task—it is important to remain objective.

A Legacy to the Future

Mexico, the United States and the international community are aware that this is an ongoing struggle. Illegal drugs continue to be harvested, no matter how many fields we destroy. New drug cartels are formed as fast as we dismantle them, corruption undermines our police forces as inexorably as moisture destroys walls, and drug consumption figures don't come down, notwithstanding multimillion budgets and investments in advertising campaigns to deter drug addiction.

The future does not look bright, but doing nothing would be our greatest failure. If we let down our guard, our young people will suffer. They will feel the full force of the drug threat, and our national security and public health will be at the mercy of organized crime.

Mexico and the United States have before them a challenge of international proportions and must continue to act in a coordinated manner, bilaterally and multilaterally, while observing their respective laws and sovereignty. And we must face other threats within our borders, such as: corruption, vested interests, pressures for drug legalization and social indifference.

> *"Mexico and the United States have before them a challenge of international proportions and must continue to act in a coordinated manner."*

Sadly, it is to be expected that thousands of children and young people will continue to die due to drugs, and billions of dollars will have to be spent before we can begin to see the fruits of our work. Moreover, there will likely be more friction between our countries on the drug issue before the binational strategy is able to partially meet its goals. This is due, in part, to our diverging national and interagency interests. However, there is nothing else we can do but continue waging this war without quarter, with all the human and financial resources at our disposal and with political determination.

Fighting against the scourge of drugs will be our legacy to future generations. We can not foresee whether we will be successful or not, but it would be cowardly to not even try.

Drug Prohibition Is Counterproductive

by David Boaz

About the author: *David Boaz is the executive vice president of the Cato Institute, a libertarian think tank in Washington, D.C.*

Ours is a federal republic. The federal government has only the powers granted to it in the Constitution. And the United States has a tradition of individual liberty, vigorous civil society, and limited government: just because a problem is identified does not mean that the government ought to undertake to solve it, and just because a problem occurs in more than one state does not mean that it is a proper subject for federal policy.

Perhaps no area more clearly demonstrates the bad consequences of not following such rules than drug prohibition. The long federal experiment in prohibition of marijuana, cocaine, heroin, and other drugs has given us unprecedented crime and corruption combined with a manifest failure to stop the use of drugs or reduce their availability to children.

A Failure Then and Now

In the 1920s Congress experimented with the prohibition of alcohol. On February 20, 1933, a new Congress acknowledged the failure of alcohol Prohibition and sent the Twenty-First Amendment to the states. Congress recognized that Prohibition had failed to stop drinking and had increased prison populations and violent crime. By the end of 1933, national Prohibition was history, though in accordance with our federal system many states continued to outlaw or severely restrict the sale of liquor.

Today Congress confronts a similarly failed prohibition policy. Futile efforts to enforce prohibition have been pursued even more vigorously in the 1980s and 1990s than they were in the 1920s. Total federal expenditures for the first 10 years of Prohibition amounted to $88 million—about $733 million in 1993 dollars. Drug enforcement cost about $22 billion in the Reagan years and another $45 billion in the four years of the Bush administration. The federal government

Excerpted from testimony given by David Boaz to the U.S. House of Representatives, Government Reform and Oversight Committee, Subcommittee on Criminal Justice, Drug Policy, and Human Resources, June 16, 1999, Washington, D.C.

spent $16 billion on drug control programs in FY [fiscal year] 1998 and has approved a budget of $17.9 billion for FY 1999. The Office of National Drug Control Policy reported in April 1999 that state and local governments spent an additional $15.9 billion in FY 1991, an increase of 13 percent over 1990, and there is every reason to believe that state and local expenditures have risen throughout the 1990s.

Those mind-boggling amounts have had some effect. Total drug arrests are now more than 1.5 million a year. There are about 400,000 drug offend-

> *"The long federal experiment in prohibition of marijuana, cocaine, heroin, and other drugs has given us unprecedented crime and corruption."*

ers in jails and prison now, and over 80 percent of the increase in the federal prison population from 1985 to 1995 was due to drug convictions. Drug offenders constituted 59.6 percent of all federal prisoners in 1996, up from 52.6 percent in 1990. (Those in federal prison for violent offenses fell from 18 percent to 12.4 percent of the total, while property offenders fell from 14 percent to 8.4 percent.)

Hardly a Successful Policy

Yet as was the case during Prohibition, all the arrests and incarcerations haven't stopped the use and abuse of drugs, or the drug trade, or the crime associated with black-market transactions. Cocaine and heroin supplies are up; the more our Customs agents interdict, the more smugglers import. In a letter to the *Wall Street Journal* published on November 12, 1996, Janet Crist of the White House Office of National Drug Policy claimed some success:

> Other important results [of the Pentagon's anti-drug efforts] include the arrest of virtually the entire Cali drug cartel leadership, the disruption of the Andean air bridge, and the hemispheric drug interdiction effort that has captured about a third of the cocaine produced in South America each year.

"However," she continued, "there has been no direct effect on either the price or the availability of cocaine on our streets."

That is hardly a sign of a successful policy. And of course, while crime rates have fallen in the past few years, today's crime rates look good only by the standards of the recent past; they remain much higher than the levels of the 1950s.

As for discouraging young people from using drugs, the massive federal effort has largely been a dud. Despite the soaring expenditures on antidrug efforts, about half the students in the United States in 1995 tried an illegal drug before they graduated from high school. According to the 1997 National Household Survey on Drug Abuse, 54.1 percent of high school seniors reported some use of an illegal drug at least once during their lifetime, although it should be noted that only 6.4 percent reported use in the month before the survey was conducted. Every year from 1975 to 1995, at least 82 percent of high school seniors have said they find marijuana "fairly easy" or "very easy" to obtain. During that same period, according to federal statistics of dubious reliability, teenage marijuana use fell dramatically and then rose significantly, suggesting that cultural factors have more effect than "the war on drugs."

The manifest failure of drug prohibition explains why more and more people—from Baltimore mayor Kurt Schmoke to Nobel laureate Milton Friedman, conservative columnist William F. Buckley Jr., and former secretary of state George Shultz—have argued that drug prohibition actually causes more crime and other harms than it prevents.

Violating the Constitution and Causing Crime

Congress should recognize the failure of prohibition and end the federal government's war on drugs. First and foremost, the federal drug laws are constitutionally dubious. As previously noted, the federal government can only exercise the powers that have been delegated to it. The Tenth Amendment reserves all other powers to the states or to the people. However misguided the alcohol prohibitionists turned out to be, they deserve credit for honoring our constitutional system by seeking a constitutional amendment that would explicitly authorize a national policy on the sale of alcohol. Congress never asked the American people for additional constitutional powers to declare a war on drug consumers.

> *"Addicts are forced to commit crimes to pay for a habit that would be easily affordable if it were legal."*

Second, drug prohibition creates high levels of crime. Addicts are forced to commit crimes to pay for a habit that would be easily affordable if it were legal. Police sources have estimated that as much as half the property crime in some major cities is committed by drug users. More dramatically, because drugs are illegal, participants in the drug trade cannot go to court to settle disputes, whether between buyer and seller or between rival sellers. When black-market contracts are breached, the result is often some form of violent sanction, which usually leads to retaliation and then open warfare in the streets.

Our capital city, Washington, D.C., has become known as the "murder capital" even though it is the most heavily policed city in the United States. Make no mistake about it, the annual carnage that stands behind America's still outrageously high murder rates has nothing to do with the mind-altering effects of a marijuana cigarette or a crack pipe. It is instead one of the grim and bitter consequences of an ideological crusade whose proponents will not yet admit defeat.

Third, drug prohibition channels over $40 billion a year into the criminal underworld. Alcohol prohibition drove reputable companies into other industries or out of business altogether, which paved the way for mobsters to make millions through the black market. If drugs were legal, organized crime would stand to lose billions of dollars, and drugs would be sold by legitimate businesses in an open marketplace.

Fourth, drug prohibition is a classic example of throwing money at a problem. The federal government spends some $16 billion to enforce the drug laws every year—all to no avail. For years drug war bureaucrats have been tailoring their budget requests to the latest news reports. When drug use goes up, taxpayers are told the government needs more money so that it can redouble its efforts against a rising drug scourge. When drug use goes down, taxpayers are told that it would be a big mistake to curtail spending just when progress is being made. Good news or bad, spending levels must be maintained or increased.

Social Upheaval and Family Breakup

Fifth, the drug laws are responsible for widespread social upheaval. "Law and order" advocates too often fail to recognize that some laws can actually cause societal disorder. A simple example will illustrate that phenomenon. Right now our college campuses are relatively calm and peaceful, but imagine what would happen if Congress were to institute military conscription in order to wage a war in Kosovo, Korea, or the Middle East. Campuses across the country would likely erupt in protest—even though Congress obviously did not desire that result. The drug laws happen to have different "disordering" effects. Perhaps the most obvious has been turning our cities into battlefields and upending the normal social order.

Drug prohibition has created a criminal subculture in our inner cities. The immense profits involved in a black-market business make drug dealing the most lucrative endeavor for many people, especially those who care least about getting on the wrong side of the law.

Drug dealers become the most visibly successful people in inner-city communities, the ones with money, and clothes, and cars. Social order is turned upside down when the most successful people in a community are criminals. The drug war makes peace and prosperity virtually impossible in inner cities.

Sixth, the drug laws break up families. Too many parents have been separated from their children because they were convicted of marijuana possession, small-scale sale of drugs, or some other non-violent offense. Will Foster used marijuana to control the pain and swelling associated with his crippling rheumatoid arthritis. He was arrested, convicted of marijuana cultivation, and sentenced to 93 years in prison, later reduced to 20 years. Are his

> *"If drugs were legal, organized crime would stand to lose billions of dollars."*

three children better off with a father who uses marijuana medicinally, or a father in jail for 20 years?

And going to jail for drug offenses isn't just for men any more. In 1996, 188,880 women were arrested for violating drug laws. Most of them did not go to jail, of course, but more than two-thirds of the 146,000 women behind bars have children. One of them is Brenda Pearson, a heroin addict who managed to maintain a job at a securities firm in New York. She supplied heroin to an addict friend, and a Michigan prosecutor had her extradited, prosecuted, and sentenced to 50 to 200 years. We can only hope that her two children will remember her when she gets out.

Civil Liberties Abuses

Seventh, drug prohibition leads to civil liberties abuses. The demand to win this unwinnable war has led to wiretapping, entrapment, property seizures, and other abuses of Americans' traditional liberties. The saddest cases result in the deaths of innocent people: people like Donald Scott, whose home was raided at dawn on the pretext of cultivating marijuana, and who was shot and killed when he rushed into the living room carrying a gun; or people like the Rev. Accelyne Williams, a 75-year-old minister who died of a heart attack when police burst into his Boston apartment looking for drugs—the wrong apartment, as it turned out; or people like Esequiel Hernandez, who was out tending his family's goats near the Rio Grande just six days after his 18th birthday when he was shot by a Marine patrol looking for drug smugglers. As we deliberate the costs and benefits of drug policy, we should keep those people in mind.

"The drug war makes peace and prosperity virtually impossible in inner cities."

Students of American history will someday ponder the question of how today's elected officials could readily admit to the mistaken policy of alcohol prohibition in the 1920s but continue the policy of drug prohibition. Indeed, the only historical lesson that recent presidents and Congresses seem to have drawn from the period of alcohol prohibition is that government should not try to outlaw the sale of alcohol. One of the broader lessons that they should have learned is this: prohibition laws should be judged according to their real-world effects, not their promised benefits.

Intellectual history teaches us that people have a strong incentive to maintain their faith in old paradigms even as the facts become increasingly difficult to explain within that paradigm. But when a paradigm has manifestly failed, we need to think creatively and develop a new paradigm. The paradigm of prohibition has failed. I urge members of Congress and all Americans to have the courage to let go of the old paradigm, to think outside the box, and to develop a new model for dealing with the very real risks of drug and alcohol abuse. If the Congress will subject the federal drug laws to that kind of new thinking, it will recognize that the drug war is not the answer to problems associated with drug use.

Medical Marijuana

In addition to the general critique above, I would like to touch on a few more specific issues. A particularly tragic consequence of the stepped-up war on drugs is the refusal to allow sick people to use marijuana as medicine. Prohibitionists insist that marijuana is not good medicine, or at least that there are legal alternatives to marijuana that are equally good. Those who believe that individuals should make their own decisions, not have their decisions made for them by Washington bureaucracies, would simply say that that's a decision for patients and their doctors to make. But in fact there is good medical evidence about the therapeutic value of marijuana—despite the difficulty of doing adequate research on an illegal drug. A recent National Institutes of Health panel concluded that smoking marijuana may help treat a number of conditions, including nausea and pain. It can be particularly effective in improving the appetite of AIDS and cancer patients. The drug could also assist people who fail to respond to traditional remedies.

"When a paradigm has manifestly failed, we need to think creatively and develop a new paradigm."

More than 70 percent of U.S. cancer specialists in one survey said they would prescribe marijuana if it was legal; nearly half said they had urged their patients to break the law to acquire the drug. The British Medical Association reports that nearly 70 percent of its members believe marijuana should be available for therapeutic use. Even President George Bush's Office of Drug Control Policy criticized the Department of Health and Human Services for closing its special medical marijuana program.

Whatever the actual value of medical marijuana, the relevant fact for federal policymakers is that in 1996 the voters of California and Arizona authorized physicians licensed in the state to recommend the use of medical marijuana to seriously ill and terminally ill patients residing in the state without being subject to civil and criminal penalties.

Overriding Local Policy

In response to those referenda, however, the Clinton administration announced, without any intervening authorization from Congress, that any physician recommending or prescribing medicinal marijuana under state law would be prosecuted. In the February 11, 1997, Federal Register the Office of National Drug Control Policy announced that federal policy would be as follows: (1) physicians who recommend and prescribe medicinal marijuana to patients in conformity with state law and patients who use such marijuana will be prosecuted; (2) physicians who recommend and prescribe medicinal marijuana to patients in conformity with state law will be excluded from Medicare and Medicaid; and (3) physicians who recommend and prescribe medicinal marijuana to patients in conformity with state law will have their scheduled-drug DEA registrations revoked.

The announced federal policy also encourages state and local enforcement officials to arrest and prosecute physicians suspected of prescribing or recommending medicinal marijuana and to arrest and prosecute patients who use such marijuana. And adding insult to injury, the policy also encourages the IRS to issue a revenue ruling disallowing any medical deduction for medical marijuana lawfully obtained under state law.

Clearly, this is a blatant effort by the federal government to impose a national policy on the people in the states in question, people who have already elected a contrary policy. Federal officials do not agree with the policy the people have elected; they mean to override it, local rule notwithstanding—just as the Clinton administration has tried to do in other cases, such as the California initiatives dealing with racial preferences and state benefits for immigrants.

Congress and the administration should respect the decisions of the voters in Arizona and California; and in Alaska, Nevada, Oregon, and Washington, where voters passed medical marijuana initiatives in 1998; and in other states where such initiatives may be proposed, debated, and passed. One of the benefits of a federal republic is that different policies may be tried in different states. One of the benefits of our Constitution is that it limits the power of the federal government to impose one policy on the several states.

Repeal Mandatory Minimums

The common law in England and America has always relied on judges and juries to decide cases and set punishments. Under our modern system, of course, many crimes are defined by the legislature, and appropriate penalties are defined by statute. However, mandatory minimum sentences and rigid sentencing guidelines shift too much power to legislators and regulators who are not involved in particular cases. They turn judges into clerks and prevent judges from weighing all the facts and circumstances in setting appropriate sentences. In addition, mandatory minimums for nonviolent first-time drug offenders result in sentences grotesquely disproportionate to the gravity of the offense. Absurdly, Congress has mandated minimums for drug offenses but not for murder and other violent crimes, so that a judge has more discretion in sentencing a murder than a first-time drug offender.

> *"More than 70 percent of U.S. cancer specialists in one survey said they would prescribe marijuana if it was legal."*

Rather than extend mandatory minimum sentences to further crimes, Congress should repeal mandatory minimums and let judges perform their traditional function of weighing the facts and setting appropriate sentences.

A Moral and Medical Problem

Drug abuse is a problem, for those involved in it and for their family and friends. But it is better dealt with as a moral and medical than as a criminal problem—"a problem for the surgeon general, not the attorney general," as Mayor Schmoke puts it.

The United States is a federal republic, and Congress should deal with drug prohibition the way it dealt with alcohol Prohibition. The Twenty-First Amendment did not actually legalize the sale of alcohol; it simply repealed the federal prohibition and returned to the several states the authority to set alcohol policy. States took the opportunity to design diverse liquor policies that were in tune with the preferences of their citizens. After 1933, three states and hundreds of counties continued to practice prohibition. Other states chose various forms of alcohol legalization.

> *"Congress should repeal mandatory minimums and let judges perform their traditional function of . . . setting appropriate sentences."*

Congress should withdraw from the war on drugs and let the states set their own policies with regard to currently illegal drugs. The states would be well advised to treat marijuana, cocaine, and heroin the way most states now treat alcohol: It should be legal for licensed stores to sell such drugs to adults. Drug sales to children, like alcohol sales to children, should remain illegal. Driving under the influence of drugs should be illegal.

With such a policy, Congress would acknowledge that our current drug policies have failed. It would restore authority to the states, as the Founders envisioned. It would save taxpayers' money. And it would give the states the power to experiment with drug policies and perhaps devise more successful rules.

Repeal of prohibition would take the astronomical profits out of the drug business and destroy the drug kingpins that terrorize parts of our cities. It would reduce crime even more dramatically than did the repeal of alcohol prohibition. Not only would there be less crime; reform would also free police to concentrate on robbery, burglary, and violent crime.

The War on Drugs has lasted longer than Prohibition, longer than the War in Vietnam. But there is no light at the end of this tunnel. Prohibition has failed, again, and should be repealed, again.

Drug Prohibition Violates Civil Liberties

by Peter McWilliams

About the author: *Peter McWilliams is the author of numerous books, including* Ain't Nobody's Business if You Do: The Absurdity of Consensual Crimes in Our Free Country.

On December 17, 1997, I was working in my living room-office on my computer next to a fire—sort of high-tech meets Abe Lincoln. It was not yet dawn, and I had been working most of the night. Leonard Cohen's "Famous Blue Raincoat" begins, "It's four in the morning, the end of December." It's a special time of night and a special time of year. The rest of the world has gone quite mad with Christmas, and I am left alone to get some work done.

A hard pounding on the door accompanied by shouts of "Police! Open Up!" broke the silence, broke my reverie, and nearly broke down the door. I opened the door wearing standard writer's attire, a bathrobe, and was immediately handcuffed. I was taken outside while Drug Enforcement Administration (DEA) agents ran through my house, guns drawn, commando-style. They were looking, I suppose, for the notorious, well-armed, highly trained Medical Marijuana Militia. To the DEA, I am the Godfather of the Medicine Cartel. Finding nothing, they took me back into my home, informed me I was not under arrest, and ordered me—still in handcuffs—to sit down. I was merely being "restrained," I was told, so the DEA could "enforce the search warrant."

A Reasonable Search?

However, no search warrant was immediately produced. Over the next hour, one page after another of the warrant was placed on a table nearby. I was never told the reasons a federal judge thought it important enough to override the Fourth Amendment of the Supreme Law of the Land and issue search warrants for my Los Angeles home of eleven years, my new home (two doors away), and the offices of my publishing company, Prelude Press, about a mile away. The reasons, I was told, were in an affidavit "under seal."

Excerpted from "The DEA Wishes Me a Nice Day," by Peter McWilliams, *Liberty,* May 1998. Reprinted with permission.

In other words, I have no way of determining whether this is a "reasonable" search and seizure. The DEA agents could have written the judge, "We've never seen the inside of a writer's house before and we'd like to have a look. Also, those New York federal judges are very touchy about letting us go into New York publishing houses, so can we also have a look at Prelude Press here in L.A.?"

Whatever the reason, I was in handcuffs, and the nine DEA agents and at least one IRS Special Agent put on rubber gloves and systematically went through every piece of paper in my house. (Were the rubber gloves because I have AIDS, or are they just careful about leaving fingerprints?)

I should point out, as I promised them I would, that I was never "roughed up." The DEA agents were, at all times, polite, if not overtly friendly. During the three hours of their search, the DEA agents asked me tentative, curious questions about my books, as though we had just met at an autographing party. They admired my artwork, as though they were guests I had invited into my home. They called me by my first name, although I am old enough to be the father of any of them.

A DEA *Special* Agent (not just one of those worker-bee agents) made it a point to tell me that the DEA has a reputation for busting into people's homes, physically abusing them, and destroying property, all in the name of "reasonable search and seizure." This, he reminded me on more than one occasion, was not taking place during this search and seizure. I agreed, and promised to report that fact faithfully. I have now done so.

Patriots

I suppose the DEA considers this a step up, and I suppose I agree, but it was eerie to see bright (for the most part), friendly, young people systematically attempting to destroy my life. I do not use the word "destroy" lightly. DEA agents are trained to fight a war, the War on Drugs, and in that war I am the enemy—a fact I readily admit. The DEA, therefore, fights me with the only tools it has—going through my home, arresting me, putting me in jail for the rest of my life, asset-forfeiting everything I own, selling it, and using the money to hire more DEA agents to fight the War on Drugs. From these young people's point of view, invading my home is an act of patriotism.

In a DEA agent's mind, because I have spoken out against the War on Drugs, I'm not just an enemy, but a traitor. In 1993, I published *Ain't Nobody's Business If You Do: The Absurdity of Consensual Crimes in Our Free Country*. In this libertarian tome— endorsed by a diverse group including Milton Friedman, Hugh Downs, Archbishop Tutu, and Sting—I explored in some detail the War on Drugs' unconstitutionality, racism, anti-free market basis, deception, wastefulness,

"I was never told the reasons a federal judge thought it important enough to override the Fourth Amendment."

destructiveness, and un-winnability. I see it as one of the darkest chapters in American history, and certainly the greatest evil in our country today.

My view is at odds, obviously, with the last line of DEA Administrator Thomas Constantine's 1995 essay, "The Cruel Hoax of Legalization": "Legalizing drugs is not a viable answer or a rational policy; it is surrender." According to Administrator Constantine, I and "many proponents of drug legalization," are "wealthy members of the elite who live in the suburbs and have never seen the damage that drugs and violence have wrought on poor communities, and for whom legalization is an abstract concept." An abstract concept. Like life, liberty, and the pursuit of happiness.

> *"The DEA . . . fights me with the only tools it has—going through my home, arresting me, . . . [and] asset-forfeiting everything I own."*

Given my outspoken opposition to the Drug War, I shouldn't be surprised that the DEA wanted to search my home. The Drug War is another Vietnam. Most of the drug warriors know it, and they have no intention of losing this war and becoming the homeless people so many Vietnam veterans have tragically become. Smart drug warriors. So, to the DEA, I'm part of the nation's enemy. And I must admit, by DEA standards, I have been pretty bad.

But when I got sick, I got even worse.

An Outspoken Advocate

In mid-March 1996 I was diagnosed with both AIDS and cancer. (Beware the Ides of March, indeed.) I had not smoked marijuana or used any other illicit drug for decades prior to this (a decision I now regret). But since 1996 I owe my life to modern medical science and to one ancient herb.

And so I became an outspoken advocate for medical marijuana. In 1996, before the passage of California Proposition 215 (the Medical Marijuana Act), I donated office space to a cannabis club so it could sell marijuana to the sick. I also started the *Medical Marijuana Magazine* on-line in February 1997; testified in favor of medical marijuana before the California Medical Examiners Board and the National Academy of Sciences; and appeared as a medical marijuana advocate in or on numerous media, including CNN, MSNBC, *The Los Angeles Times*, Associated Press, United Press International, CBS Radio Network, and dozens more.

For a sick guy, I've been around. (Actually, I've been around, and that's how I got to be a sick guy, but that's another story.) Most disturbing to the DEA, I would guess, was my strong criticism of it in a two-page ad I placed in the December 1, 1997, *Daily Variety*. I denounced Administrator Constantine's threat to criminally investigate the creators of *Murphy Brown* for Murphy's fictional use of medical marijuana. Having made comments such as, "The DEA gives the phrase 'ambulance chasing' a whole new meaning," I'm surprised it took

51

the DEA 17 days to find my house—but, then, they are part of the government.

About two weeks before my DEA Christmas visitation, the *Medical Marijuana Magazine* on-line announced it would soon be posting portions of a book on medical marijuana that I've been working on, *A Question of Compassion: An AIDS Cancer Patient Explores Medical Marijuana*. My publishing company announced that books would ship in January. This brings us back to my computer and the DEA agents' almost immediate interest in it.

My computer and its backup drives, which the DEA also took, contained my entire creative output—most of it unpublished—for the nearly two years since my diagnosis. My central project has been the above-mentioned book and a filmed documentary with the same title. Being a fair, balanced, objective view of medical marijuana in the United States, the book is scathingly critical of the DEA.

So they took the computer, backup copies of my computer files, and most of my research materials on medical marijuana. William F. Buckley, Jr. said, "That is the equivalent of entering *The New York Times* and walking away with the printing machinery." If I don't get my computer and files back, it will take at least six months additional work to get back to where I was, and redoing creative work is disheartening at best.

Not only am I in shock from having been invaded and seeing my "children" kidnapped (writers have an odd habit of becoming attached to their creative output), but every time I go for something—from a peanut butter cup to a magazine—it's not there. Something is there, but it's not what was there 24 hours earlier. Everything reeks of nine different fragrances—like the men's cologne department at Macy's. My address books were also taken—not copied, taken. As you can imagine, all this is most disorienting, especially for a born-again marijuana addict like me.

How the DEA Works

A few random observations:

While rummaging through my publishing company, a DEA agent told the publishing staff, "You guys had better start looking for new jobs. If the DEA doesn't take this place for marijuana, the IRS will. The government will own this place in six months." Such a statement does not just have a chilling effect on a publishing company; it is like putting an iceberg in front of the *Titanic*.

"They took the computer, backup copies of my computer files, and most of my research materials on medical marijuana."

The DEA took a microcassette tape from the recorder next to my bed. On the tape I had dictated a letter to President Clinton (dictating to President Clinton in bed seemed appropriate), asking him to rise above politics and show his compassion by making medical marijuana available to the sick. I may never get to mail that letter now, but I certainly hope the DEA agent who listens to it will transcribe it and send it to his or her boss's (Constantine) boss's (Reno) boss (Clinton).

I have precisely three porn magazines in my house, hidden deep away in my sock drawer. (Who has enough socks to fill a whole drawer?) The magazines were removed from their stash and placed on top of random objects before photographing them. A jury, looking at these photographs, would think I have pornography all over the place. Frankly, I don't mind if a jury thinks this, because my view of pornography agrees completely with that of Oscar Levant: "It helps."

> *"While rummaging through my publishing company, a DEA agent told the publishing staff, 'You guys had better start looking for new jobs.'"*

When the DEA agents found a collection of *Playboys* at the offices of Prelude Press (the Playboy Forum is, in fact, one of the best anti-prohibition information sources around), I am told (as I was not there) that three of the male DEA agents spent a great deal of time testosteronistically pawing through and making typically sexist comments about portions of the magazine that have nothing to do with drugs—but that are obviously addictive nonetheless.

An invasion of nine people into the world of someone with a suppressed immune system is risky at best. DEA agents come into contact with criminals and other DEA agents from all sorts of international places with all sorts of diseases. Some of these diseases don't infect their young federal bodies, but the agents pass them along. I think of certain strains of tuberculosis, deadly to people with AIDS and rampant in certain quarters—quarters where I make it a point not to go, but quarters in which the DEA seems to thrive. Since my diagnosis, I have lived the life of a near hermit, especially during flu season, which is now. Thundering into my sterile home surrounded by the clean air of Laurel Canyon is the equivalent of germ warfare. At least two of the agents were sniffling or coughing. Six of them handled me in some way. I kept flashing back to the U.S. Cavalry passing out smallpox-infested blankets to shivering Native Americans. Have these people no sense of the struggle AIDS sufferers have in fighting even ordinary illnesses, and the lengths some of us go to avoid unnecessary exposure to infection? (Naive American question, huh?)

Prospects

Philosophically, or at least stoically, one could say all this is part of my research into medical marijuana and those who oppose it—especially into those who oppose it. The problem is that I'm not sure what I've learned. Two scenarios surface, each more frightening than the other.

Scenario One: The DEA, angered by my criticism and fearful of more, decided to intimidate me—and to have a free peek at my book in the bargain.

Scenario Two: In July 1997, the DEA invaded the home of a man named

Todd McCormick, destroyed his marijuana research plants (one of which had been alive since 1976), took his computer (which had notes for a book he is writing), and has not yet returned it. Perhaps the DEA—caught in a blind, bureaucratic feeding frenzy—is just now, five months later, getting around to investigating my connection as possible financier of Todd's "Medical Marijuana Mansion" or even—gasp!—that I grew some marijuana for myself. This means that in order to justify the arrest of Todd McCormick, a magnificent blunder, they are now coming after me, a magnificent blunder.

Whichever scenario is correct, if the DEA and IRS have their way I may spend the rest of my life in a federal prison, all expenses paid (and deaths from AIDS-related illnesses can be very expensive, indeed). Truth be told, prison doesn't particularly frighten me. All I plan to do the rest of my life is create things—write, mostly. I've been everywhere I want to go. It's my time of life for didactic pontificating. It is a phase writers go through immediately preceded by channel surfing and immediately followed by channel surfing. Or hemlock.

If the DEA has seized my computer to silence me, it has failed, as I hope this article illustrates. The DEA's next oppressive move, then, would be to arrest me.

(Some have cautioned me about assassination, which I find difficult to comprehend—but then I thought my book was so safe I didn't even have a backup in a Public Storage locker somewhere. I should, I suppose, state that I am not in any way suicidal about this—or anything else, for that matter. So if I should die before the DEA wakes and they claim my death was a suicide, don't you believe it. I plan to go about as quietly into that good night as Timothy Leary did. Still, as a naive American, this concern is far from my mind.)

If the DEA intends to come after me as the financier of Todd McCormick's medical marijuana empire, the DEA knows full well I took credit for that immediately after Todd's arrest—which made a lie of the DEA's claim that Todd purchased his "mansion" with "drug money." Yes, I gave him enough money to rent the ugliest house in Bel-Air and, being Todd McCormick, he grew marijuana there. The money I gave him was an advance for a book on cultivating marijuana.

Todd cannot use medical marijuana as a condition of his bail-release. He is drug-tested twice weekly. He cannot go to Amsterdam where he could legally find relief from the pain of cancer. Todd now faces life imprisonment—a ten-year mandatory minimum—and a $4 million fine, for cultivating medical marijuana, which is specifically permitted under the California Compassionate Use Act of 1996.

> *"If the DEA has seized my computer to silence me, it has failed. . . . The DEA's next oppressive move, then, would be to arrest me."*

The DEA, at the federal level, and California Attorney General Dan Lungren (with Governor Pete Wilson smiling his approval from on high) should have opposed Proposition 215 in court. In court they had the right—and the responsibility, if they truly believed it a bad law—to challenge the law and ask a judge to stay its enactment. They did not. Instead, the DEA is fighting its War on Drugs in the sickrooms of Todd, me, and countless others.

Our government is not well.

What Our Patriots Are Doing Today

As I write this, I feel myself in mortal combat with a gnarly monster. Then I remember the human faces of the kind people who tried to make me comfortable with small talk as they went through my belongings as neatly as they knew how.

It reminds me, painfully, that the War on Drugs is a war fought by decent Americans against other decent Americans, and that these people rifling through my belongings really are America's best—bright young people willing to die for their country in covert action. It takes a special kind of person for that, and every Republic must have a generous number of them in order to survive.

> *"Our misguided government is using all [its] talent to harass and arrest Blacks, Hispanics, the poor, and the sick—the casualties in the War on Drugs."*

But instead of our best and our brightest being trained to hunt down terrorist bombs or child abductors—to mention but two useful examples—our misguided government is using all that talent to harass and arrest Blacks, Hispanics, the poor, and the sick—the casualties in the War on Drugs, the ones who, to quote Leonard Cohen again, "sank beneath your wisdom like a stone." It is the heart of the evil of a prohibition law in a free country.

After all, picking on someone with AIDS and cancer is a little redundant, don't you think?

On the way out, one of the DEA agents said, "Have a nice day."

I believe the comment was sincere.

Drug Prohibition Is Unfair to Minorities

by Jesse Jackson

About the author: *Jesse Jackson, a reverend and longtime civil rights activist, is president and founder of the Rainbow/PUSH (People United to Save Humanity) Coalition, an organization dedicated to expanding economic, political, and educational opportunities for disadvantaged communities.*

America's war on drugs is a debacle with ever-increasing casualties and costs. The prison population has tripled since 1980 because the law requires jail time for drug offenders. Even so, drug use continues to rise among the young and stay roughly the same overall.

Americans do not use more drugs, on average, than people in other nations, but the U.S. alone has chosen to lock up low-level offenders. Nearly 60 percent of all people in federal prisons are doing time for drug violations. In state and local jails, the figure is 22 percent. And more than a third of all of them are locked up for simple possession of an illicit drug.

"America's internal gulag," is what Gen. Barry McCaffrey, the nation's drug czar, calls the growing collection of drug inmates.

Targeting Minorities

For years, the drug war focused on one drug crack cocaine, and one target young, urban, males, disproportionately black and Hispanic. Crack is simply cocaine processed so it can be smoked. But federal laws equates 5 grams of crack with 500 grams of powder cocaine. Possessing 5 grains of crack cocaine is a felony with an automatic five year prison term; the same amount of the same drug in powder form gets you a misdemeanor with no time at all.

The perverted law is reinforced by racially targeted enforcement. Twice as many whites as blacks use crack, and three times as many whites as blacks use powder cocaine. Yet nearly 90 percent of the people locked up for crack under federal drug laws are African Americans. In state prisons, blacks are nearly 60 percent of those serving time on drug offenses, according to Justice Department figures, even though they are only 15 percent of regular drug users.

McCaffrey argues that we didn't "get into this fix because of racism." Enforcement is concentrated on the inner-city neighborhoods where crack is a scourge.

So those neighborhoods are targeted and, as the killings from New York City to Riverside, Calif., have shown, too often terrorized by police.

> *"For years, the drug war focused on . . . one target— young, urban males, disproportionately black and Hispanic."*

This war at home was fed by hysteria in the mid 1980s. Crack was labeled "America's drug of choice," by NBC News. William Bennett, peddling fear for self-promotion as President George Bush's drug czar, warned crack might soon invade every home in America. It was, according to *Newsweek*, the "most addictive drug known to man."

In reality, crack was never close to the most popular drug in America. Alcohol and tobacco turned out to be more addictive. Ten years of national surveys have shown that most people who try the drug do not continue to use it.

Harsh Laws

But the hysteria helped bring about laws with mandatory prison sentences, pumped billions into building new prisons, and militarized local law enforcement agencies, aided by surplus military equipment handed over at the end of the Cold War. The war on drugs went from metaphor to description.

Now, a prison/industrial complex of enormous power has been built. States are spending $35 billion a year to arrest, prosecute and lock up drug users. Across the country, the equivalent of a new 1,000 bed jail opens every week. States like California started spending more on state prisons than on state universities and colleges.

Gen. McCaffrey argues that the "current system is bad drug policy and bad law enforcement." He says dealing with the drug menace is "more akin to dealing with cancer" than to fighting a war. The Sentencing Commission revealed that of the people jailed by the federal government for crack offenses, only 5 percent were considered high-level dealers. Prosecutors and judges—even conservative Supreme Court Chief Justice William Rehnquist—have called for cutting back on mandatory sentences and returning discretion to the courts.

But the war on drugs continues, undaunted by failure. The reason: politics and pork.

Dr. James Alan Fox, dean of the college of criminal justice at Northeastern University, summarizes: "For politicians, the drug debate is driven by the three Rs—retribution, revenge, retaliation—and that leads to the fourth R, re-election."

Every time McCaffrey tries to bring a touch of reason to the debate, Republicans scream that the administration is soft on drugs. And the White House immediately jumps to show how tough it is. It even overturned its own Sentencing Commission's recommendation to change the discriminatory crack cocaine sentencing laws.

For years, the hawks have argued that the war on drugs is for the benefit of "the most vulnerable among us, the residents of our inner cities," as House Crime Subcommittee Chairman Bill McCollum (R-Fla), a man not otherwise known for his concern for the urban poor, puts it. Yet today, the war itself is destroying lives and wasting billions of dollars that might otherwise be spent on schools and treatment.

It is time to help the general end the war. Let's lock in treatment for the sick, not lock out hope.

The U.S. Should Not Pressure Other Countries to Comply with Its Prohibition Efforts

by Hal Jones

About the author: *Hal Jones is editor in chief of* Harvard International Review.

Many policymakers in Washington believe that the United States can use its role as the hegemonic power in the hemisphere to induce its neighbors to launch extensive campaigns against the production and trafficking of illegal narcotics. Since 1986, for example, the US Congress has required the president to assess the performance of Latin American nations in the war on drugs. If the efforts of the drug-producing country are judged to be insufficient, the US government "decertifies" that nation and cuts off aid. What US officials fail to realize is that the strength or weakness of Latin American anti-drug efforts is determined not so much by the level of pressure exerted by the United States as by Latin American policymakers' assessments of how potential courses of action will affect the perceived legitimacy of their government. The behavior of the Mexican government between 1970 and 1985 and the actions of the Peruvian government in the 1980s demonstrate that Latin American states will respond favorably to US pressure only when such a reaction is in accord with their interest in asserting national sovereignty.

Defending Mexican Sovereignty

Mexico carried out intensive and largely successful anti-drug campaigns in the 1970s and early 1980s primarily because Mexican leaders realized that such efforts would enhance the legitimacy of the government and increase the administration's effective control over the country's territory. To be sure, the zeal

Excerpted from "The Limits of Pressure: U.S. Policy Failures in the International War on Drugs," by Hal Jones, *Harvard International Review*, Spring 1998. Reprinted with permission from the *Harvard International Review*.

with which Mexico pursued its *campaña permanente* ("permanent campaign") against drugs pleased US officials, who supported the initiative with equipment and advice. However, Mexico's anti-drug program represented an attempt to address internal challenges to Mexican sovereignty much more than an effort to placate the country's powerful neighbor to the north.

> *"Latin American states will respond favorably to US pressure only when [it] is in accord with their interest in asserting national sovereignty."*

One factor that led the Mexican government to take decisive action against illegal drug activity was the decline of governmental authority in the states of Sinaloa, Durango, and Chihuahua, which formed a vast "critical triangle" in the northwestern part of the country. There, drug producers grew marijuana and poppies, and *narcotraficantes* set up operations in defiance of the central government. Because these criminal elements effectively exercised control over large areas of practically inaccessible national territory, Mexican leaders realized that a protracted and energetic effort would be necessary to reassert the authority of the central administration. They subsequently designed an ambitious campaign to meet the challenge. Surely pressure from Washington was not necessary to convince officials in Mexico City of the need to reclaim sovereignty over the increasingly lawless regions dominated by drug traffickers.

A related concern was the fear that anti-government insurgencies would find support and a secure base of operations in the drug-producing areas of the northwest. Indeed, some Mexican officials apparently worried that guerrilla movements were already active there. Thus, moving against drug rings was seen as a way to eliminate an even greater threat to national sovereignty than that posed by the drug traffickers themselves. Moreover, Mexican leaders reasoned that the experience gained by the military in fighting the war on drugs would be valuable as counterinsurgency training even if no guerrillas were found to be operating in drug-producing areas.

Mexico's government also perceived an internal threat to its security from drug traffickers in that it recognized a growing drug abuse problem among its own citizens. Therefore, an effort to reduce domestic consumption was made as a part of the country's anti-drug campaign. The United States had no direct interest in the realization of this goal and is unlikely to have applied pressure to coerce its neighbor into pursuing such policies. Thus, the Mexican administration's domestic priorities appear to have been more important than the values of the US government in determining many of the areas upon which the *campaña permanente* focused.

The Limits of US Pressure

Some scholars have argued that Mexico's energetic anti-drug initiative in the 1970s was primarily the result of pressure applied by the United States through the Nixon administration's short-lived Operation Intercept. Initiated in 1969, the operation briefly interrupted the flow of goods and people between the two countries. These observers point to the apparent "pressure-response" pattern of US-Mexican relations that was established as early as the 1940s and that seems to have endured to the present day. In the judgment of these authors, "Mexico responds to American pressure more out of need than shared perception of the problem."

However, it would be misleading to accept the explanation that US pressure was the most important force leading the Mexican government to launch the *campaña permanente*. Because of Mexico's historical experience as a victim of what it perceives as US aggression, the country's leaders often implement policies that are at odds with the interests of the US government. For example, Mexico was unique among Latin American countries in its refusal to sever diplomatic ties with Cuba. By defying the will of the United States, Mexican policymakers enhance their domestic political standing by appearing to act as guardians of the country's independence from US power.

Therefore, because of the domestic political costs involved, Mexican officials are unlikely to implement a policy that coincides with US interests unless the policy in question also clearly serves an important Mexican interest. Few Mexican interests could be as important to policymakers in that country as the revered principle of national sovereignty, which even 150 years after the Mexican-American War serves as the basis for the country's hesitance to support multilateral pro-democracy missions in the Organization of American States. Because the Mexican government realized that national sovereignty was at stake in the war against drugs—and not directly as a result of US pressure—officials in Mexico City moved decisively against the production and trafficking of illicit narcotics beginning in 1970.

> *"The Mexican administration's domestic priorities appear to have been more important that the values of the US government."*

The Peruvian Case

The irrelevance of US pressure to the formation of anti-drug policies in Latin America is seen even more clearly in the context of the Peruvian experience. During much of the 1980s, Peruvian leaders, in contrast to their Mexican counterparts, largely neglected the fight against drugs despite US pressure to act more vigorously. US efforts failed to induce the Andean nation to launch aggressive anti-drug efforts primarily because the Peruvian government calculated that anti-narcotics campaigns would undermine the legitimacy and sovereignty of the central government by making it more difficult to contain a violent and dangerous insurgency.

In 1984, the Peruvian government suspended its anti-narcotics activities in the coca-producing Upper Huallaga Valley in order to confront the threat to its authority posed by the Shining Path guerrillas who controlled much of the area. Because the vast majority of the local population was involved in the coca trade, unpopular crop eradication and drug interdiction programs had to be scaled back and then stopped so that the military could win the support of the people for its counterinsurgency campaign. As early as January 1984, the Peruvian army was hampering the efforts of anti-drug police agencies. When the valley was designated as an emergency zone on July 10 of that year, General Julio Carbajal banned counter-narcotics operations in the area altogether.

Not only did Carbajal allow local farmers to continue producing coca, he also forged contacts with powerful drug traffickers who provided intelligence in return for the general's non-interference in their activities. The United States was understandably annoyed that the anti-drug programs it had helped to start were being abandoned and that Peruvian officials were actually supporting illegal drug activity. The US government in 1984–85 therefore attempted to apply pressure through its embassy to convince the Peruvians to adjust their counterinsurgency strategy and to reactivate the fight against narcotics. However, those efforts failed as long as the Shining Path remained active because both the central government and the military leadership saw the guerrillas as a far greater threat to national sovereignty and security than drug trafficking.

Balancing Priorities

In the late 1980s, as well, after the Upper Huallaga Valley had again become an important base for Shining Path activities, the Peruvian government ignored US pressure to do more about drug trafficking and instead placed a higher priority on neutralizing the guerrillas. In April 1989, Peru's leaders again declared the region to be an emergency zone, and they charged General Alberto Arciniega with the task of eliminating the danger presented by the Shining Path.

As Arciniega knew from his US-provided training, counterinsurgency operations in a disturbed area had to have the support of the local population to be successful. Therefore, the general sought to convince the people of the region that the army was on their side, and to that end he maintained a ban on anti-drug campaigns. Crop substitution was encouraged, but coca eradication efforts were stopped because Arciniega believed that "each *campesino* who was attacked would

> *"Mexican officials are unlikely to implement a policy that coincides with US interests unless [it] also clearly serves an important Mexican interest."*

become, the next day, one more *senderista* [Shining Path supporter]." The United States reacted angrily to Arciniega's failure to fight drugs while simultaneously fighting guerrillas, and US officials pressured the Peruvian government to change its policies. Arciniega retained the support of President Alan García, however, and he remained at his post until December 1989, by which time he was able to declare that the Upper Huallaga Valley had "ceased to be a disturbed area."

Not the Result of Pressure

In an attempt to argue that US pressure did have a major impact on Peruvian anti-drug policies, observers of that country's recent history might point out that the government in Lima did move relatively quickly to lift the state of emergency in the Upper Huallaga Valley and to re-institute counter-narcotics efforts. The anti-drug initiatives suspended by the military in mid-1984, for example, were re-launched and intensified in the second half of 1985. Similarly, Arciniega's departure from the drug-producing region after just nine months in command marked the end of the period during

> *"During much of the 1980s, Peruvian leaders . . . largely neglected the fight against drugs despite US pressure to act more vigorously."*

which Peruvian authorities prevented the operations of anti-drug forces. However, it was not US pressure but rather the effectiveness of the military effort in the valley and the civilian government's fear of the rise of a popular military leader that led officials in Lima quickly to rescind the emergency provisions under which counter-narcotics operations were banned.

One explanation for the fact that the periods of emergency rule in 1984–1985 and 1989 were rather short is that the military was at least temporarily successful in its efforts to eliminate the threat posed by the Shining Path to the integrity of the nation. Control over the Upper Huallaga Valley was taken out of the hands of the generals not because they had failed to pursue policies that pleased officials in Washington but because they had accomplished their tasks. By April of 1985, the Peruvian government was confident that the army had "guarantee[d] peace for the population." Similarly, by the time he was relieved of his post in late 1989, General Arciniega could assert that terrorist activity in the region had been "substantially reduced." Both the US State Department and General Arciniega denied that North American pressure had anything to do with the brevity of his tenure in the valley.

The government might have been particularly anxious to transfer its successful generals out of the area quickly because civilian leaders feared the emergence of powerful military figures who could present a challenge to their authority. Having been overthrown by military officers in 1968, President Fernando Belaunde (1963–1968, 1980–1985) certainly had reason to fear such an outcome. Likewise, President García (1985–1990), who had promised during his campaign to reduce the power of the military, must have worried that Arciniega was building a power base in the valley when 60,000 people hailed the general as a hero in a November 1989 rally. These domestic factors explain the relatively short duration of military rule in the Upper Huallaga Valley.

The speed with which Peru returned to anti-drug efforts afterwards can be accounted for with reference to President García's apparent moral opposition to drugs. US officials may have approved of García's anti-narcotics stance, but the Peruvian leader's nationalistic, anti-US ideology makes it unlikely that his political position on the drug issue was influenced by Washington.

A Counterproductive Policy?

As the cases of Mexico and Peru demonstrate, US attempts to pressure Latin American countries into adopting more vigorous anti-drug policies tend to be ineffectual. Far more important to Latin American policymakers are their calculations of how a particular approach to the drug problem would affect their efforts to guarantee the authority, sovereignty, and integrity of their national governments. If Latin American officials do decide to pursue anti-drug policies that are in accord with US interests, the cause will more likely be a result of those calculations rather than a result of coercive North American measures.

Not only should US policymakers recognize that their heavy-handed tactics tend to be ineffective, but they should also admit that such policies can be counterproductive. When Latin American officials are trying to develop policies that enhance the legitimacy and sovereignty of their national government, an option that is being thrust upon them by a powerful nation that has a long tradition of interfering in the region will be decidedly unattractive.

Mexico Is Not Committed to Cooperation with U.S. Drug Prohibition Efforts

by Scott Park

About the author: *Scott Park is a writer for the* Dallas Morning News *and* Human Events *newspapers.*

On February 27, 1999, President Clinton officially declared the government of Mexico recertified as a cooperating partner in the war on drugs. The declaration was about as accurate as the President's deposition in the Paula Jones case.

Being certified as a partner in the war on drugs qualifies Mexico to receive U.S. foreign aid and trade benefits. In February 1999, for example, the administration announced that the U.S. Export-Import Bank will give Mexico $4 billion in export financing-money Mexico could not get if it was not recertified.

In March 1999, at a hearing of his Senate Appropriations Subcommittee on Commerce, Justice, State and the Judiciary, Chairman Judd Gregg (R.-N.H.) dared to contradict Clinton on the certification issue. "It's hard to understand how Mexico can be certified," said Gregg, "because there has been no significant progress in stopping drug-trafficking, and many of the categories, in fact most of the categories are poor."

"Seizures of cocaine and heroin have fallen significantly," he said. "Drug arrests have declined by 14%. The number of poppy fields destroyed and drug laboratories dismantled has dropped. This is all in 1998.

"Confiscation of drug-carrying cars, trucks and boats has declined. Seizure of opium gum has declined by just over half since 1997. Corruption continues to pervade the law enforcement community to the point where the DEA [Drug Enforcement Administration] has serious reservations about even dealing with the law enforcement community in Mexico."

Atty. Gen. Janet Reno was forced to agree with Gregg, and testified on March

Excerpted from "Clinton's Mexican Drug Policy Is a Certifiable Fraud," by Scott Park, *Human Events,* March 19, 1999. Reprinted with permission from the author.

9, 1999, that "the picture you paint of corruption and problems in Mexico is one that we have all shared and have expressed frustration on."

The President Turns a Blind Eye

Declaring that Clinton has turned a "blind eye" to Mexico City's real record on drug-trafficking, Rep. Spencer Bachus. (R.-Ala.) has introduced a bipartisan resolution to decertify our southern neighbor.

"The drug lords operating in Mexico fear only one thing: extradition to the United States, where they will face punishment for their crimes. That doesn't happen nearly enough in Mexico," said Bachus.

But the most damning assessment of Mexico's performance comes from the man who knows the most about it: Tom Constantine, director of the Drug Enforcement Administration. Constantine told Congress that Mexican nationals, directed by the major drug cartels, are now operating drug distribution networks throughout the United States. The DEA is now arresting Mexican drug dealers in U.S. cities that Americans are unaccustomed to associating with big-league drug crimes—places such as Greensboro, N.C., and Des Moines, Iowa.

Two-thirds of the cocaine sold in the United States now comes across the Mexican border. But that's not all:

Mexican marijuana dominates the U.S. market. In 1991, 102 metric tons were seized in the United States. In 1998, 742 metric tons were seized. In Boise, Idaho, DEA agents arrested a group of illegal aliens carrying 114,000 marijuana plants that weighed almost 20 tons.

> *"Mexican nationals, directed by the major drug cartels, are now operating drug distribution networks throughout the United States."*

It is also now common to find Mexican nationals peddling methamphetamines in American communities. In Iowa, health experts found that of the 4,000 infants affected by drugs, 90% had been exposed to methamphetamine.

Mexico produces 14% of the heroin sold in the United States and transships roughly a third.

Bribery and Violence

U.S. intelligence agencies believe the drug cartels spend $1 million per day bribing Mexican officials to keep the drug corridors to the United States open. Mexican drug lords also use violence to intimidate authorities they can't bribe, and they are beginning to employ the same practices in the U.S. Many U.S. law officers in the border area have been targeted.

In the first 11 months of 1998, Mexican drug lords were suspected to have been responsible for 54 incidences of violence or threats of violence against U.S. and Mexican officials. These were just the latest episodes in an ongoing and escalating pattern.

Since September 1996, the DEA has recorded 141 incidents of violence against U.S. officials, Mexican officials and informants on the border or in Mexico.

Since 1992, in the border land of Cochise County, Ariz., there have been 23 documented threats or assaults against law enforcement officers.

In 1998, traffickers began shooting at U.S. Border Patrol agents who chased them back into Mexico.

On June 3, 1998, a U.S. Border Patrol agent was murdered by Mexican marijuana traffickers on U.S. territory.

> *"U.S. intelligence agencies believe the drug cartels spend $1 million per day bribing Mexican officials."*

Two days after Christmas 1998, two Mexican drug fighters were snatched from the street in Matamoras, Mexico. On January 8, 1999, their corpses turned up outside Brownsville, Tex. They had been tortured and executed.

"Even at the zenith of their power, American organized crime leaders did not wield the power and influence that the international drug-trafficking organizations do at this time," said Constantine.

Corruption of Mexican Officials

When the U.S. government tries to train Mexican drug fighters, the effort usually fails because each time the Mexicans launch a new uncorrupted agency or unit to fight the drug trade, it soon becomes obvious to U.S. officials that the cartels have penetrated the new entity. Critical drugfighting evidence and intelligence has been leaked to the cartels through such Mexican agencies.

In June 1998, four Mexican drug officials were caught providing "security" for tractor trailers driving north loaded with marijuana.

In October 1998, two elite Mexican officials allowed a major trafficker to escape for $38,000.

In February 1998, a Mexican commander charged with directing investigations into drug-related murders and kidnappings was fired. He was discovered to be aligned with the cartel leader he was ostensibly investigating.

Also in February 1998, the chief of public safety for the Mexican state of Baja was arrested. He and three other police officers provided security for a 17-ton shipment of Colombian cocaine being off-loaded at an airstrip.

In 1997, Mexico began using its military to fight drugs because corruption was so pervasive in its civil law agencies. But the military hasn't located or arrested any drug lords, and U.S. officials now fear that the military, too, is compromised.

Coming Up Short

In 1997, Congress took up, but failed to pass, a resolution to decertify Mexico if it didn't improve its anti-drug performance. It did, however, pass a resolution that listed steps Mexico would need to take to be judged as cooperating.

Mexico has come up short in taking these steps, said Rep. John Mica (R.-Fla.). "The entire western portion of Mexico south of the U.S. and California is now run by one of the drug cartels. Completely corrupt, complete controlled," he said.

"We've also been told that the Yucatan peninsula has been taken over by narco-terrorists," said Mica. Mexico also failed to honor these congressional requests: Allow DEA agents to carry firearms, and extend them appropriate immunities (after U.S. agents uncovered widespread corruption among Mexican bankers, Mexico threatened to indict our border agents).

Root out corruption and extradite major drug-traffickers. "Not one major drug-trafficker had been extradited to the U.S.," said Mica. There are 150 outstanding extradition requests.

Sign a maritime agreement allowing the U.S. to pursue dealers into Mexican waters.

Place radar sites in the south of Mexico to monitor shipments coming north.

Replace corrupt officials with honest drug fighters. Mexico is so rife with corruption it's impossible to trust any agency, said Mica.

> *"Each time the Mexicans launch a new uncorrupted agency or unit . . . , it soon becomes obvious . . . that the cartels have penetrated the new entity."*

When Mica asked the General Accounting Office (GAO) whether Mexico was cooperating, the GAO said, "Mexico is one of the largest centers of narcotics-related business in the world." It is also, said the GAO, a major hub in the recycling of drug proceeds.

"The certification law is quite simple," said Mica. "It asks two requests: Stop producing drugs; stop transiting in drugs.

"The Department of State and the President must certify to Congress that a country is cooperating fully to do those two things."

The question to Congress, said Mica, is to determine if Mexico is fully complying. The evidence clearly shows that "they are the biggest source of deadly drugs and narcotics coming in to the United States."

Chapter 2

Should U.S. Drug Policies Be Liberalized?

The Politics of Drug Policy Reform: An Overview

by Erich Goode

About the author: *Erich Goode is professor of sociology at the State University of New York at Stony Brook and the author of* Between Politics and Reason: The Drug Legalization Debate.

The political landscape is a maze of contradictions; politics, we are told, make for "strange bedfellows." Perhaps nowhere is this more apparent than in the issue of drug legalization. In a letter to the editor to *The New York Times*, anti-drug crusader William Bennett charged the pro-legalization forces with being "strange bedfellows." What Bennett does not say is that advocates of all positions on the drug legalization question crawl under the sheets with ideologies they would reject in other areas. Positions that are very close to one another in general may actually have drastically differing views on drug policy; likewise, positions that seem poles apart on most other issues may snuggle up on the question of what to do about drugs. Here, the distinction between advocates of legalization and prohibitionists are frequently fractured by cross-cutting political views. Seen politically, positions on legalization may be regarded as the secondary manifestation of deeper and more compelling ideological commitments.

Dividing the Drug Legalization Pie

To be specific about it, most conservatives oppose a relaxation of the drug laws, but many extreme conservatives favor a program of complete decriminalization; at the other end of the spectrum, many radicals oppose certain forms of legalization as state control, and in that view, agree with many extreme conservatives, who propose something of a laissez-faire policy. Black politicians, usually well at the liberal end of the political spectrum, are (with a tiny number of exceptions) staunchly opposed to drug legalization. Moving toward the center, advocates of legalization (taken as a whole) and prohibitionists (again, lumped together) stand on opposite sides of the great divide on the issue of legalization, but a more nuanced view of their positions suggests that "progressive" advo-

Excerpted from "Strange Bedfellows: Ideology, Politics, and Drug Legalization," by Erich Goode, *Society,* May/June 1998. Copyright ©1998 by Transaction Inc. Reprinted with the permission of Transaction Publishers.

cates of legalization and "progressive" prohibitionists share much more in common than the first does with the more extreme or "hard core" advocates of legalization and the latter does with the more extreme or "hard core" prohibitionists. Consequently, the usual political spectrum is not a very useful road map for finding out where someone stands on drug policy.

"Advocates of all positions on the drug legalization question crawl under the sheets with ideologies they would reject in other areas."

How do we divide up the drug legalization debate pie? What are the most prominent positions on this issue? Who stands where on the question of legalization? Peter Reuter made use of a warfare analogy in locating "doves," "hawks," and "owls." In limning the ideological landscape of the debate over what to do about the drug problem, Franklin Zimring and Gordon Hawkins find generalists (those who apply the same standards to all psychoactive substances, regardless of their legal status), legalists (who say a drug is what the law says is a drug), and cost-benefit specifists (pragmatists who set aside issues of morality and consider only harm reduction). Ethan Nadelmann, an outspoken, prolific, and high-profile advocate of legalization, delineates "legalizers, prohibitionists, and the common ground," suggesting that some adherents of positions on either side of this divide may share more with one another than with their presumed allies. What sort of "strange bedfellows" perplexities do we find spread across the drug legalization canvas?

The more high-profile views on the drug legalization issue may be crystallized out as follows: cultural conservatives; free trade libertarians; radical constructionists; progressive legalizers; and progressive prohibitionists.

Traditional Values

Cultural conservatives. Cultural conservatives believe in "old fashioned" values; they feel that what is wrong with the country, drug abuse included, is that too many people have strayed too far from age-old custom and tradition. We should return to mainstream religion; the traditional family; conventional sexual practices; the "basics" in education; strong communities where neighbors care about one another; conformity to traditional values; moderation in our consumption of alcohol; complete abstention from illegal psychoactive substances; and so on. What is bad about the country is that there is too much freedom, rampant individuality, hedonism, selfishness, a lack of concern for our fellow human beings, godlessness, lack of a communitarian spirit, a too-heavy reliance on the federal government to do things for us, not enough self-control—all of which lead to divorce, abortion, pornography, illegitimacy, crime, violence, and drug abuse. . . .

Cultural conservatives adopt what Zimring and Hawkins refer to as a legalistic definition of drugs and drug abuse: A drug is an illegal psychoactive substance, and drug abuse is use of a drug outside a medical context. Advocates of legalization draw a sharp distinction between alcohol, on the one hand, and all currently illegal drugs, on the other; alcohol is not a drug, nor is alcoholism a type of drug abuse. For the cultural conservative, drug abuse is immoral, a repugnant vice. (So is the immoderate abuse of alcohol, although, again, it does not qualify as drug abuse.) By its very nature, indulgence in drugs degrades human life. Drugs should be outlawed because using them represents a repudiation of the status quo—that is, tradition, conservative values, all that is good and true. Intoxication represents an unhealthy decadence, an expression of degeneracy, a quest for a spurious, insidious, ill-gotten, illegitimate pleasure. It is incompatible with a decent life; drug intoxication and the decent life are a contradiction in terms. . . .

Promoting Zero Tolerance

The answer to the drug problem for the cultural conservative, then, is a return to traditional values. Law enforcement is seen as an ally in this struggle. Victory cannot be achieved without government intervention, and that means, mainly, long sentences for violations and increased allocations for the police and for building jails and prisons. There should be "zero tolerance" for drug use—zero tolerance in the schools, the workplace, the government sector, on the highway, in the street, in public, even in the home—anywhere and everywhere intervention is feasible. If private parties can bring this about, so much the better, but the government must be enlisted in this fight because it has the resources, the power, and the influence to exert a major impact.

> "*Cultural conservatives adopt . . . a legalistic definition of . . . drug abuse: . . . drug abuse is use of a drug outside a medical context.*"

Cultural conservatives have a great deal of faith in the "War on Drugs"; Richard Nixon, Ronald Reagan, and George Bush all used the expression often and were zealous generals in this "war." Carrying on this tradition in his campaign speeches, presidential candidate Bob Dole vowed to re-ignite the drug war, which had lapsed, he claimed, under Bill Clinton—whom he designated politically and culturally far to his left. More specifically, cultural conservatives have a great deal of faith in a principle we might refer to as absolute deterrence. That is, they do not believe simply that law enforcement is more likely to "contain" or keep a given activity in check or at a lower level than no enforcement at all; instead, they argue, that war can—absolutely—defeat the enemy. Further, they believe (or, at least, in their speeches and writings, they state) that law enforcement, if not restrained by loopholes, technicalities, and restrictions, will actually reduce that activity, ideally, nearly to zero. We can win the war on drugs, the cultural conservative asserts, if we have sufficient will, determination, and unity. . . .

Chapter 2

Laissez-Faire Decriminalization

Free-market libertarians. Both cultural conservatives and free-market libertarians are at the conservative end of the political spectrum, but they disagree on almost everything else pertaining to drug legalization. For one thing, while cultural conservatives believe that there are real differences between legal and illegal drugs, free-market libertarians believe that the legal-illegal distinction is artificial and should be dismantled. Technically, free-market libertarians are opposed to legalization, but for exactly the opposite reason as the cultural conservatives. While the cultural conservatives feel that legalization would represent a dangerous step toward too little government intervention and control, for the free-market libertarian, legalization would result in too much government intervention and control. The libertarian wants a laissez-faire or "hands off" government policy—no government-administered methadone maintenance programs, no government "drug stores" or "supermarkets," no Alcohol Beverage Control package stores, no laws telling citizens what they can and can't do, no medical prescriptions for imaginary neuroses or mental illnesses, no restrictions, controls, legislation, or regulations whatsoever.

No one should be forced to take drugs, they say, and no one should be forced not to take drugs. One major exception for many in this camp—a condition for which a law is necessary—is the age of the purchaser: An adult should not be allowed to sell drugs to a minor. Otherwise, more or less "anything goes." What free-market libertarians want is complete decriminalization, not state-controlled, state-supervised legalization. Psychiatrist Thomas Szasz and economist Milton Friedman stand foursquare in this tradition; their coauthored volume, *On Liberty and Drugs*, contains a chapter, penned by Friedman, entitled "The Drug War as a Socialist Enterprise." Interestingly, they also believe that legalization would represent a "socialist enterprise.". . .

An America Free of Drug Laws

For the free-market libertarians, the fundamental point is that drugs represent a form of property; they feel that the ownership of property is sacred, not to be tampered with by the government in any way. Only under extremely limited circumstances does the government have the right to step in and take away such a basic and fundamental right. Under most circumstances, they believe, where such restrictions are practically nonexistent, the public good will be maximized. . . . There are very few instances, many free-market

> *"Cultural conservatives have a great deal of faith in the 'War on Drugs.'"*

libertarians feel, where this principle is so blatantly violated as with the drug laws. And legalization is not much better, they believe; it simply results in ever more state intervention. To the free-market libertarian the ideal solution is complete decriminalization of currently illegal drugs.

Free-market libertarians do not delude themselves into thinking that decriminalization will eliminate either drug use or the medical harm that drug use causes; to them, this is beside the point. But they do believe that instilling a sense of personal responsibility in a citizenry for their own actions is more likely to result in them choosing the most reasonable path than if the government forces them to do something against their will, or prevents them from doing what they might otherwise choose to do. Such paternalism breeds the very dependency that we (mistakenly) attribute to drugs. Our aim should not be, in Thomas Szasz's words, a "drug-free America" but an "America free of drug laws." In the 19th century, there were no legal controls on drugs; in our century, we must "return to a free market in drugs. We need not reinvent the wheel to solve our drug problem. All we need to do is to stop acting like timid children, grow up, and stand on our own two feet."

> *"What free-market libertarians want is complete decriminalization."*

Drug Abuse as a Symptom of Inequality

Radical constructionists. To some degree, all social scientists are constructionists; all of us are interested in how interpretations of reality are constructed, what functions they serve, how they grow out of broader political and ideological views, and what consequences they have. However, these days, some of us seem to be arguing that the brute facts of the material world count for very little in these social and cultural constructs, that almost any interpretation of reality can be dished up and accepted as true, no matter how much it may run counter to the facts, if it serves the interests of certain privileged segments of the society. Observers with these views could be called radical constructionists. Radical constructionists are not so much in favor of legalization as opposed to the "war on drugs." They argue that, objectively speaking, there is no real drug crisis. The government has targeted drugs and drug users because they serve as a convenient scapegoat: Most are poor and powerless, many are members of racial and ethnic minorities, they do not have the resources with which to fight back, or they are members of a despised, stigmatized deviant category, and hence, they are inconvenient for the affluent, hegemonic segments of the society. Attention to the phony drug "crisis" serves the function of diverting attention away from the real problems of the day—problems which either cannot be solved within the existing institutional framework or which, if they were solved, would snatch privileges away from the affluent, the powerful, and the privileged. . . .

Radical constructionists do not see drugs as the enemy. Most argue that drug abuse is the symptom of a problem, not the cause of it. The problem is, of course, the gross inequity in society's resources: poverty, unemployment, urban decay, the powerlessness of the poor and racial minorities, racism, a lack of

economic opportunities in the inner cities, combined with the grotesque afflu-
ence of the very rich. Drug selling, at least at the street level, is caused not by a
character flaw but by a lack of economic opportunity; drug abuse is not an expression of being weak-willed but of hopelessness brought on by urban decay.

The solution to the drug problem is not legalization by itself, which will do
nothing to solve the ills and injustices of poverty or the grossly unfair distribution of society's resources. Clarence Lusane, in *Pipe Dream Blues* writes: "As
long as economic and racial inequities exist, abuse will continue whether drugs
are legal or illegal." Hence, a "radical redistribution of wealth" and "fundamental economic reform" must be at the heart of any meaningful response to the
drug crisis. After this, more crucial but less grandiose measures must be taken.
High on any reform agenda: "establishing new approaches to policing and law
enforcement." Communities must take back their streets; the police must listen
to and be responsive to the needs of the people, and discontinue stereotyping,
stigmatizing, and harassing poor, inner city minorities. Alternatives to prison
must be instituted, such as community service; prisons are already over-
crowded, and African-Americans are hugely over-represented—and growing—
in the prison population. The "war on drugs" should cease. Law enforcement
should stop criminalizing the junkie; drug addiction should be seen as a
medical not a criminal matter. Treat-ment facilities, especially those that
involve the community and are drug-free, should be hugely expanded. At
the same time, high-level dealers who conspire to poison poor and mi-

> *"Radical constructionists do not see drugs as the enemy. Most argue that drug abuse is the symptom of a problem, not the cause."*

nority communities should be handed long prison sentences. In conjunction
with these changes, alcohol and tobacco could be restricted in a variety of
ways; their sale is profitable to their manufacturers and harmful disproportionately to the poor. Above all, what is needed is empowerment—a vastly greater
and more effective participation in the political process by the poor, the under-
represented, and members of racial and ethnic minorities. With empowerment
will come economic redistribution which, in turn, will bring about a defeat of
drug abuse as a major problem in American society.

Drug Addiction as a Health Problem

Progressive Advocates of Legalization. Unlike the cultural conservatives, progressive advocates of legalization are generalists; they hold a definition of
drugs that is based on their psychoactive quality, not their legality. In fact, such
advocates wish to dismantle or at least radically restructure the legal-illegal distinction. Unlike the free-market libertarian, the progressive advocate of legalization does believe in state control of the dispensation of psychoactive substances. Unlike the radical constructionist, the progressive advocate of

legalization argues that the drug laws are the problem. Matters of reforming the economy, the political system, and redistributing society's resources are important in themselves, but the reform of drug policy, too, is a crucial issue in its own right. Progressive advocates of legalization are more concerned with what to do about drugs than about reformulating the political and economic system generally. They think that there are many things that are seriously wrong with the present system, but that the laws prohibiting drugs represent one of them; they wish to reform them, so that there will be less pain and suffering in the world.

> *"Progressive advocates of legalization believe that most of the harms from the use of currently illegal drugs stems from criminalization."*

How does the progressive formulate or frame the drug legalization issue? What is the nature of the drug problem, and what is the solution? For the most part, progressive advocates of legalization see the drug problem as a human rights issue. What they are talking about when they discuss drug reforms is treating drug addiction as a health problem, much like schizophrenia or alcoholism—not as a crime or law enforcement problem. Above all, society should, in Ethan Nadelmann's words, "stop demonizing illicit drug users"; "they are citizens and human beings." Criminalizing the possession and use of the currently illegal drugs is unjust, oppressive, and inhumane; it has no moral justification. It represents a kind of witch-hunt, and it penalizes the unfortunate. Innumerable young lives are being ruined by imprisonment for what are essentially victimless crimes. It is the suffering of the drug user that is foremost on the progressive's mind in demanding a reform of drug policy. Nadelmann, the progressives' foremost and most well-known spokesperson concludes: "Harm reduction means leaving casual drug users alone and treating addicts like they're still human beings." "My strongest argument for legalization," he adds, "is a moral one. Enforcement of drug laws makes a mockery of an essential principle of a free society—that those who do no harm to others should not be harmed by others, particularly by the state. . . . To me, [this] is the greatest societal cost of our current drug prohibition system.". . .

Contrasting Progressive Legalizers and Prohibitionists

The position of progressive advocates of legalization can best be appreciated by a contrast with that of the progressive prohibitionists. Advocates of both positions urge reforms in the drug laws, both are, or claim to be, concerned with harm reduction, both attempt to weigh costs and benefits carefully and empirically in any evaluation of drug policy, and both believe that users of the illegal drugs are treated too harshly, and that the legal drugs are too readily available. But the differences between these two positions are as important as their similarities.

There are three major and profound dissimilarities between the progressive advocates of legalization and the progressive prohibitionists: First, in their evaluation of costs and benefits, progressive advocates of legalization weigh the moral values of individual liberty, privacy, and tolerance of the addict very heavily, while the progressive prohibitionist to some degree sets these values aside and emphasizes concrete, material values—specifically public health— much more heavily. Second, in considering the impact of legalization—more specifically, whether it will increase use or not—progressive advocates of legal- ization are optimists (they believe that use will not increase significantly), while progressive prohibitionists are pessimists (they believe that use will increase, possibly even dramatically). Even if use does increase, the progressive advo- cates of legalization say, legalization is likely to result in increased use of less harmful drugs and decreased use of more harmful substances.

And third, progressive advocates of legalization believe that most of the harms from the use of the currently illegal drugs stems from criminalization, while the progressive prohibitionists believe that such harms are more a product of use per se than of the criminalization of those drugs. Harm from contami- nated drugs, the grip of organized crime, the crime and violence that infects the drug scene, AIDS, medical maladies from addiction—all secondary, not pri- mary effects of drugs. And all will decline or disappear under legalization. Pro- gressive prohibitionists are skeptical. With very few exceptions, progres- sive advocates of legalization have not spent a great deal of time or space spelling out what their particu- lar form of legalization would look like. Still, they do not mean by legal- ization what free-market libertarians

> *"Most progressive advocates of legalization realize that selling drugs in a kind of 'supermarket'. . . is not feasible."*

mean by decriminalization, nor, indeed, what their critics mean by legalization. "When we talk about legalization, we don't mean selling crack in candy stores," says Nadelmann. Unlike free-market libertarians, most progressive advocates of legalization realize that selling drugs in a kind of "supermarket," where any and all psychoactive substances would be as readily available as heads of lettuce and cans of soup, is not feasible for the foreseeable future. Many point to harm reduction strategies that seem (to some observers) to have worked in the Netherlands, Switzerland, and England. All support steps in that direction: le- galize or decriminalize marijuana, increase methadone maintenance programs, reschedule many Schedule I drugs (such as LSD, ecstasy, and heroin) that may have therapeutic utility, stop arresting addicts, get them into treatment pro- grams, and so on. However, they see these as only stopgap or transitional steps. If not the supermarket model, then what would full legalization look like? Nadelmann suggests that the mail order model might work: sell drugs in limited quantities through the mail. While not the ideal solution, it is the best compro- mise "between individual rights and communitarian interests." It must be noted that, while all progressive advocates of legalization emphasize the unanticipated consequences of prohibition, they do not spend much time or space considering the possible unanticipated consequences that legalization itself might have.

A Communitarian Position

Progressive prohibitionists. Progressive prohibitionists (such as Mark Kleiman, Mark Moore, Franklin Zimring, and Gordon Hawkins), urge many of the same reforms that progressive advocates of legalization argue for; most of them, for instance, would support most of the following: needle exchange, condom distribution, an expansion of methadone maintenance, no incarceration of the addict, rescheduling of many Schedule I drugs, a consideration of legalization or decriminalization of marijuana, higher taxes and more controls on alcohol and tobacco. (Interestingly, as I said, there are far more similarities between progressive prohibitionists and progressive advocates of legalization than there are between the former and "hard-line" criminalizers on the one hand, and between the latter and "radical" or "extreme" free-market libertarians, on the other.) The progressive prohibitionists draw the line, however, at the legal, over-the-counter or even mail-order sale of drugs such as heroin, cocaine, and amphetamine.

Progressive prohibitionists are not as distressed by the moral incongruity of criminalizing the possession and sale of powerful psychoactive agents and legally tolerating substances or activities that also cause harm. Once again, to demarcate their position from that of the progressive advocates of legalization, they say, to some degree, there is a special and unique quality in certain drugs that compels some users of them to become abusers. Not a majority of the society, they say, but a sufficient minority to warrant concern for the public health of the entire society. In fact, to step back and look at their political, ideological, and moral position more generally, progressive prohibitionists are far more communitarian than individualistic. While the touchstone of the progressive advocate of legalization is the rights of the individual, for the progressive prohibitionist, the guiding principle is the health of the community. The individual, they would say, does not have the right to harm the society; certain rights have to be curbed for the good of the society as a whole. If injured, the individual has to be cared for by the community; foolish acts engaged in by the individual are purchased at the price of a very substantial cost to the rest of us. The individual does not have the legal or moral right to ignore the seat belt laws, the helmet laws, or rules and regulations against permitting him or her to be placed in extreme danger— or any other laws, rules, or regulations that attempt to protect individuals from harming themselves. Any humane society must balance freedom over and against harm, and in this equation, quite often, certain freedoms must be curtailed. In short, compared with progressive advocates of legalization, pro-

> *"For the progressive prohibitionist, the guiding principle is the health of the community."*

78

gressive prohibitionists are much more concerned with a potential gain in public health than with the moral issue of which human rights are, allegedly, abridged. For instance, coercing addicts and drug abusers into drug rehabilitation programs by arresting them and giving them a choice between imprisonment and treatment is not a moral problem for the progressive prohibitionist as it would be for the progressive advocate of legalization. . . .

An Ideological Debate

Again, while the more progressive prohibitionists and the more moderate or progressive advocates of legalization share many items in their drug policy agenda, they differ on these three major issues: how much they stress individual liberty versus public health; their prediction of whether drug abuse, and its attendant harms, will increase significantly under legalization; and their notion of whether the currently illegal drugs are more intrinsically or directly harmful or harmful indirectly, that is, mainly because they are illegal. Ironically, although the progressive advocates of legalization and the progressive prohibitionists stand on opposite sides of the great legalization divide, they share more particulars of their drug policy proposals than any two major positions in this debate. If major changes in drug policy do take place in the next century, they are likely to be drawn from the substantial overlap in these two positions.

The various approaches to drug legalization fit more or less comfortably into, and have relevance and resonance for, quite distinct political views or orientations. Drug legalization may be said to be a specific instance of, or a specific issue for, a more general political, ideological, and moral position. The issue is thought about in terms of a broader image or world-view expressing how things ought to be. In this sense, then, it is misleading to think about the debate strictly in pragmatic or empirical terms. In many ways, it is an ideological debate about which political perspective will dominate policy on drugs in the years to come.

Drug Policies Should Be Liberalized

by Hank Kalet

About the author: *Hank Kalet is the news editor for two central New Jersey weekly newspapers.*

The war on drugs is, simply, a war on sanity. It is a failed policy of prohibition, focused primarily on urban blacks and Latinos, that has done little more than fill our jails, overtax our police departments and turn an entire population of addicts into criminals.

It has created an underground economy that thrives on violence and greed, an economy that appears to offer those who enter its maze instant gratification and riches, but more often than not leaves its participants dead or in jail.

And it has resulted in dangerous attacks on our civil liberties through the use of neighborhood drug sweeps, the denial of housing to the families of drug dealers, motor vehicle stops made based on the color of the driver's skin and eased search and seizure rules.

We spend about 70 percent of all federal anti-drug money on law enforcement and the control of our national borders, crafted mandatory sentencing laws that punish nonviolent offenders with years and years of hard time crowding our jails and destroying generations.

The drug war is a policy driven by the belief that taking a hard line on drugs is what sells during political elections, that candidates who do not get behind the latest anti-drug gimmick will be swept from office by someone tougher and meaner.

Changing Public Opinion

Perhaps things are changing. Voters in six states and the District of Columbia indicated their willingness to take a different tack when they approved measures allowing the use of marijuana for medical purposes. All told, voters in seven states and D.C., which account for about one-fifth of the electorate, have now endorsed "medical marijuana," despite widespread opposition from local,

Excerpted from "Stop the War," by Hank Kalet, *Progressive Populist*, March 1999. Reprinted with permission.

state and federal office-holders and the law enforcement community. [In fact, Congress forbade the release of the final vote in the District of Columbia.]

Ethan Nadelmann, director of the Lindesmith Center drug policy institute, told William Greider in the Dec. 24, 1998 issue of *Rolling Stone* that the referenda will put pressure on elected leaders to find a different approach to drug abuse and use.

"We spend about 70 percent of all federal anti-drug money on law enforcement and the control of our national borders."

"Those politicians who thought there was no cost to indulging in drug-war demagoguery may now find themselves in an argument with their own voters," he told Greider. "They don't want to face up to that, but the American people will no longer be duped by such inflammatory language."

The medical-marijuana movement, Greider points, was led by an array of public health workers and those stricken by AIDS and cancer and their families.

"I saw I had to prescribe marijuana for my patients, and I saw that it worked," hospice physician Rob Killian of Seattle told Greider. "All drugs have a dangerous side, but as physicians, we are trained to administer pharmaceuticals in a safe, appropriate manner. My patients who are suffering and dying are not criminals."

The results are an indication that voters are willing to move beyond the what Eva Bertram and Kenneth Sharpe have called "a dead-end, partisan debate over who stands tougher against drug use and dealing." (*The Nation*, Jan. 6, 1997)

Government Resistance

Unfortunately, those who've been waging America's "War on Drugs" do not appear ready to listen. The president and his administration repeatedly have turned a deaf ear to the medical marijuana argument, promising to prosecute health-care professionals who suggest their patients may benefit from smoking marijuana. And while the administration has said it will listen if scientific evidence is presented that shows marijuana to have therapeutic benefits, it has allowed studies of the drug to be stymied by politics.

"They speak in two different voices," Nadelmann told Greider. "One ridicules medical marijuana, the patients and doctors. The other approach is to say, 'Let the science prevail.' Yet any time the medical-marijuana studies come up through their system of scientific review and gain legitimacy, they are cut off by political decisions."

Restoring Sanity

There are alternatives to the current madness—some of which have been endorsed by some influential members of the law enforcement and public health communities—alternatives that could go a long way toward restoring safety to our streets and sanity to our lives.

These reforms include legalization of marijuana and the decriminalization of other drugs, free and open access to treatment and needle exchange programs. Their advocates say these efforts can "reduce the harmful consequences of drug use to the individual, his or her loved ones and the community as a whole" (Bertram and Sharpe)—which ultimately should be the guiding principal of U.S. drug policy.

The alternatives look like this:

• Legalize pot. Marijuana is a relatively harmless drug that has a mellowing effect on those who use it and has few addictive properties. Turning those who use the drug into criminals makes no sense and it keeps the drug out of the hands of cancer and AIDS patients and those who suffer from epilepsy and other nervous system disorders.

There is a load of evidence that shows that using marijuana helps cancer and AIDS patients maintain their weight and their strength, which in turn helps their bodies fight off infections and viruses. And it also aids them in avoiding mood swings. There also is anecdotal evidence that suggests the drug has a salutary effect on patients who suffer from epilepsy and other nervous system disorders.

Legalization—which would bring with it government controls—also would guarantee a safe supply of marijuana that is free of contaminants and of a known and consistent potency and price, rather than force

> *"There are alternatives . . . that could go a long way toward restoring safety to our streets and sanity to our lives."*

users to deal with the underground economy. This is similar to the way that alcohol, tobacco and over-the-counter and prescription drugs are regulated.

And there would be the added bonus of drug tax revenue.

Decriminalization, Treatment, and Free Needles

• Decriminalize other drugs, with strict controls on their use. This would include the various opiates, which already are used by physicians to control pain; the various cocaine derivatives; psychedelics, amphetamines and barbiturates. By decriminalizing these drugs, we could reduce the role of the criminal in their distribution and take the illicit profit out of their sale, while regulating their potency and purity.

Tied to this would be free and open access to treatment facilities for addicts seeking to turn their lives around.

• Make free needles available to intravenous drug users to help slow the spread of AIDS and other infectious diseases.

As Bertram and Sharpe point out, more than a third of all AIDS cases are associated with intravenous drug use. "Passed on through the sharing of contaminated needles, the AIDS virus is contracted each year by 10,000 drug users, their sex partners and their children—the equivalent of one to two preventable HIV infections per hour, including the majority of AIDS cases in children under 13."

Needle-exchange programs (NEPs), which provide sterile needles to addicts and encourage them to seek treatment, have been implemented across the country. And according to Bertram and Sharpe, "Mounting evidence demonstrates that NEPs can significantly slow the spread of AIDS and do not encourage increased drug use."

Not a Criminal Issue

• Alter the way we view drug abuse and drug-abuse prevention. We need to start looking at drug addiction as a public health issue, as we do alcoholism and AIDS, and not as a criminal issue.

This means educating the public with real information, not the scare tactics that generally pass for drug education in this country.

People need to understand the physiological effects of various drugs—including those over-the-counter remedies and prescription medications we seem to be addicted to—and the very real pleasures that these drugs can provide. People need to understand both the ups and the downs of toking on a joint, shooting up or knocking back a shooter of Jack Daniels, and they need to understand that the downside can be far greater than the upside.

As former Secretary of State George Schultz has said, "We're not really going to get anywhere until we take the criminality out of the drug business and the incentives for criminality out of it."

Drugs Should Be Legalized

by Dirk Chase Eldredge

About the author: *Dirk Chase Eldredge is the author of* Ending the War on Drugs: A Solution for America.

America's war on drugs is reminiscent of the Russian princess who wept profusely at the death of the hero in the opera, while, at the curb, her waiting carriage driver froze to death in a cruel Moscow ice storm. Policy makers are deeply preoccupied with waging the war on drugs. While they do, the destructive, albeit unintended, consequences continue to pile up like the icy snows of Moscow.

The world would be a much better place if illicit drugs didn't exist, but they do, so we must deal with them. Our challenge is to do so in a way that will advance our national interest. Our failed war on drugs is doing just the opposite; America must respond to that reality with a basic change in approach.

The Only Practical Way

Legalization is the only practical way to bring about positive results. The money legalization would generate to fight drug abuse would make harm reduction—rather than the twice-failed policy of prohibition—the fulcrum of our drug policy. The failure of prohibition as public policy stems from its transformation of some citizens' cocktail-hour-like drug use and others' medical and psychological problems into crimes. It is no less devastating than if we made both possession and consumption of alcoholic beverages illegal. Social drinkers and alcoholics alike would suddenly be criminalized.

As it always does, prohibition has spawned a robust black market that inevitably has spun off other social pathologies such as violence and corruption. Furthermore, it is a policy that can only fail because its objective—a drug-free America—is unrealistic and unattainable.

Supporters of the drug war allege that we are winning, citing as proof a decline in drug use from the peak years of the 1970s, but that drop came to an abrupt end in 1992. The number of regular users has increased each year since then among several age groups.

Many argue against the decriminalization of drugs on the grounds that more people would abuse drugs than under prohibition. This politically popular theory is unsubstantiated and misleading. Within any group there are a certain number prone to abuse of mind-altering substances. This propensity for abuse has everything to do with the individual's personal value system and psychological stability and absolutely nothing to do with the legal status of drugs.

> *"Legalization is the only practical way to bring about positive results."*

Legalizing currently illegal drugs will neither increase nor decrease the number of people inclined toward, or indulging in, addictive behavior.

Those inclined to addictive behavior have that inclination independent of the law of the land and have ample opportunity to obtain drugs under existing laws and customs. They have two major mind-altering alternatives available that are legal: prescription drugs and alcohol. A third alternative is illegal drugs.

Legalization Will Not Increase Drug Abuse

What effect will legalization have on the abuse of drugs? To answer that question intelligently we must understand that drug use is not necessarily drug abuse. The try-and-die concept promoted by the drug warriors simply does not square with the facts. The vast majority of drug users fall into the recreational category. For instance, less than 1 percent of those who try cocaine become daily users, and 74 percent of regular cocaine users use it less than once a month. Looked at in the context of these facts instead of the hysteria promoted by the defenders of the status quo, it is not surprising that three different studies have shown only 2 to 4 percent of respondents would try now-illegal drugs if they were legalized. Given the small percentage of drug users who lapse into abuse, this hardly suggests that legalization will trigger a mass movement into drug abuse. Legalization re-asserts the truth that we are all responsible for our own behavior.

The drug war, while barren of results, is rich in ironies. For example, increased law-enforcement pressure on smuggling encourages more concentrated drugs, leading to less bulk and reduced chance of discovery. Some recent samples of heroin are 90 percent pure, compared with 7 to 15 percent purity a few years ago. This greater potency has added to heroin's popularity, exactly the opposite of what law enforcement intends, because heroin is by far the most dangerous street drug.

The Lessons of Prohibition

Our national amnesia over alcohol prohibition destines us to repeat an unintended consequence from that era. During Prohibition, the consumption of lower-potency alcoholic beverages, such as beer, plummeted while the market share of moonshine and other strong distilled spirits soared. Soon after repeal, the consumption patterns of both high- and low-potency beverages returned to pre-Prohibition levels. From this experience, we can extrapolate that today's shift to more-potent drugs is directly related to drug prohibition.

Prohibition dictates that illicit drugs only can be obtained via the black market. Prices are whatever the market will bear, resulting in high prices and obscene profits. Because drugs are so expensive, many users recruit friends to become users so they can sell drugs to them and help defray their own costs. In fact, 70 percent of those who deal drugs also are users. This results in the drug market's version of a Mary Kay network. Think for a moment about the size and motivation of the resulting drug-sales force which would immediately be immobilized by legalization.

One of the most damaging aspects of the drug black market is the allure of the easy money it makes available to our inner-city youth. A 16-year-old from Washington, virtually unemployable after having been arrested 12 times, manages to clear the heady sum of $300 to $400 a day selling crack. "I don't want to make this a life thing," he alleges. "I'll quit when I get out of high school." He then makes a telling and contradictory admission: "But when you start you really can't stop. The money is too good."

With drugs, corruption is the cancer and money the carcinogen. The corruption of public officials—police, judges, border and prison guards, customs inspectors and others in positions of public trust—is a destructive consequence of our prohibitionist drug policies. Bribery corrupts far and wide. A law-enforcement officer can provide protection against arrest. A drug-cash-laden defendant can purchase perjured testimony or bribe a judge. The wide availability of drugs inside even our most secure prisons is powerful testimony to the corruption drug money can buy.

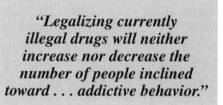

"Legalizing currently illegal drugs will neither increase nor decrease the number of people inclined toward . . . addictive behavior."

And America is exporting this corruption. Ask the police officials of Mexico, Colombia and other source countries. American narco dollars pay for drug-related murders, kidnappings and bribery in those countries. Instead of owning up to the fact that our demand is the real cause of the problem, we try to export the blame as well. We indulge in the arrogant charade of certification, judging whether other nations are doing their part in fighting the drug problem, when we should be focusing on solving the problem, whose root cause lies directly at our feet. Without our demand there would be no supply.

The Threat to Civil Liberties

Misdirected public policy, always clad in the armor of good intentions, carries with it the very real threat of repression wrought by the frustration-repression cycle of its own failure. As various drug-war tactics such as asset seizure and

mandatory minimum sentences fail, policy makers can justify ever more desperate measures. The tight spiral of initiation, failure and more-desperate measures inevitably results in a creeping loss of civil liberties.

In response to the rising pitch of drug-war hysteria during the 1980s and
1990s, 28 states passed laws to tax the possession of illegal drugs, an idea that
does violence both to the principle of fair taxation and respect for the rule of
law. We have government declaring it
illegal to possess marijuana and cocaine while simultaneously demanding payment of a tax for possession,
a clear violation of the constitutional
protection against self-incrimination.
Despite court decisions overturning
the laws, many states, most notably

> *"Think . . . about the size*
> *and motivation of the*
> *resulting drug-sales force*
> *which would immediately be*
> *immobilized by legalization."*

North Carolina, have tweaked their statutes to skirt the law and go right ahead
collecting the tax. Not coincidentally, police and sheriff's departments get 75
percent of the take. This leads to the mixing of law enforcement with the profit
motive, a recipe rife with opportunities for abuse. But never mind the danger to
our civil liberties. This is war.

Because drug dealing and use are victimless crimes, the police must either
personally observe the crime or participate in it in undercover mode to make a
valid arrest. This makes drug-law enforcement doubly labor intensive. Those in
law enforcement routinely estimate that more than half of today's crimes are
drug-related, leading to the imprisonment of over 1 million citizens per year for
drug-related crimes. This, in turn, has resulted in 40 states being placed under
court order to end prison overcrowding.

A major cost of the drug war is the corrosive effect it is having on the confi-
dence of black Americans in their government. A 1990 opinion poll of African-
Americans in New York City showed 60 percent gave partial or full credence to
the ludicrous charge that government deliberately makes sure drugs are easily
available in poor, black neighborhoods in order to harm black people.

Real Progress

As demonstrated by the social pathologies enumerated above which derive directly from prohibition, like the Russian princess, America is so preoccupied
with the show of prohibition it is oblivious to what is going on in the real
world.

By legalizing drugs and selling them for about half the present prices through
state-operated retail outlets similar to those in the 13 states that presently have
state-controlled alcohol sales, we could produce profits of conservatively $21
billion per year to fund harm reduction. This money would be required, by law,
to be used to buy the drugs for resale, run the outlets and fund treatment on demand ($12 billion), an anti-drug education program equal in cost to the com-

bined advertising budgets of the big-three auto makers ($3.25 billion) and an AIDS-sized research budget ($1.3 billion) to find pharmacological solutions to drug addiction and dependence.

This would advance the national interest by making real progress against the drug problem, not through fear, coercion and incarceration, but through education, treatment and research.

Liberalizing Drug Policies Would Reduce Crime and Violence

by New York County Lawyers' Association Drug Policy Task Force

About the author: *The New York County Lawyers' Association Drug Policy Task Force was established in 1993 to study drug policy issues and formulate a set of recommendations for resolving problems related to drug laws and drug abuse.*

It has become a widely accepted fact that drug policy, as employed during the past three decades by the federal government, and in state and local jurisdictions throughout the United States, has largely failed to meet its stated objectives.

Current drug policy relies on an "enforcement" or "penal" model, emphasizing interdiction, arrest, prosecution and incarceration of both distributors and users of controlled substances as its primary "weapons" in what has often been characterized as a "war on drugs." Commonly known substances generally designated as "controlled" or illegal include: hallucinogens (marijuana, hashish, mescaline and LSD), stimulants (amphetamines and cocaine), and depressants (opium, heroin and barbiturates).

Failures in the Drug War

Notwithstanding the vast public resources expended on the enforcement of penal statutes against users and distributors of controlled substances, contemporary drug policy appears to have failed, even on its own terms, in a number of notable respects. These include: minimal reduction in the consumption of controlled substances; failure to reduce violent crime; failure to markedly reduce drug importation, distribution and street-level drug sales; failure to reduce the widespread availability of drugs to potential users; failure to deter individuals from becoming involved in the drug trade; failure to impact upon the huge profits and financial opportunity available to individual "entrepreneurs" and organized underworld organizations through engaging in the illicit drug trade; the

Excerpted from *Report and Recommendations*, by the New York County Lawyers' Association Drug Policy Task Force, October 1996. Reprinted with permission.

expenditure of great amounts of increasingly limited public resources in pursuit of a cost-intensive "penal" or "law-enforcement" based policy; failure to provide meaningful treatment and other assistance to substance abusers and their families; and failure to provide meaningful alternative economic opportunities to those attracted to the drug trade for lack of other available avenues for financial advancement.

Moreover, a growing body of evidence and opinion suggests that contemporary drug policy, as pursued in recent decades, may be counterpro-

> *"Contemporary drug policy appears to have failed, even on its own terms, in a number of notable respects."*

ductive and even harmful to the society whose public safety it seeks to protect. This conclusion becomes more readily apparent when one distinguishes the harms suffered by society and its members directly attributable to the pharmacological effects of drug use upon human behavior, from those harms resulting from policies attempting to eradicate drug use.

With aid of these distinctions, we see that present drug policy appears to contribute to the increase of violence in our communities. It does so by permitting and indeed, *causing* the drug trade to remain a lucrative source of economic opportunity for street dealers, drug kingpins and all those willing to engage in the often violent, illicit, black market trade.

Meanwhile, the effect of present policy serves to stigmatize and marginalize drug users, thereby inhibiting and undermining the efforts of many such individuals to remain or become productive, gainfully employed members of society. Furthermore, current policy has not only failed to provide adequate access to treatment for substance abuse, it has, in many ways, rendered the obtaining of such treatment, and of other medical services, more difficult and even dangerous to pursue.

Alternative Models Must Be Considered

The appropriate goal of any drug policy must be to decrease the prevalence and spread of harmful drug use and substance abuse, and to minimize the harms associated with such problems where they are found to exist. Additionally, any policy which creates more harmful results than the societal problems it proposes to solve, must be re-evaluated in terms of the advisability of further pursuit of such policy. Further, to justify continuation of any public policy, the costs incurred must always be weighed against the benefits derived. It is within this context, and with these criteria in mind, that present approaches to drug policy must be objectively assessed and, where appropriate, alternative models for future policy evaluated and considered.

In making its assessment, the Task Force has concluded that contemporary drug policy has failed by virtually every objective standard. Accordingly, we call for a dramatic shift in thinking and approach in development and implementation of future drug control efforts. At this time, although not recommending "decriminalization" or "legalization" of most substances currently designated as "controlled" under federal and state penal statutes, the Task Force does urge that certain incremental steps be taken to alleviate the more easily resolved economic and social costs associated with current drug policy. These include: the decriminalization of marijuana; further measures attempting to separate the "hard" drug markets (e.g., for heroin and cocaine), from markets for "soft" drugs (e.g., marijuana and hashish); the downward modification of existing draconian sentences for other non-violent drug offenses; the elimination of mandatory minimum sentences in drug cases; and increased judicial discretion in the sentencing of drug offenders, with further reliance upon drug treatment and other diversionary programs as alternatives to incarceration for the non-violent drug offender. Moreover, we highly recommend the further study and serious consideration of other alternative, non-criminal, regulatory drug control measures, developed in accordance with a "public health" rather than a "penal" model of drug policy. . . .

Drug Prohibition Causes Violence

There exists a large and growing body of respected opinion and credible evidence which suggests that contemporary drug policy has failed to deter or reduce the prevalence of violent crime in our communities, notwithstanding harsh treatment of drug offenders under present "penal" or "law enforcement" based policy. Indeed, many observers have concluded that the current form of "drug prohibition" has *generated* a great deal of violence, much of it armed violence encountered in the lucrative underworld drug industry, and some deriving from law enforcement efforts themselves in the "war on drugs".

In analyzing these issues, we take great care to distinguish between violence caused by actual *drug use or substance abuse* ("drug-induced" violence), and violence caused as a byproduct of the high stakes involved in the illicit drug trade ("drug trade" or "drug prohibition" related violence). This distinction is critical, because unless the causes of crimes and violence are accurately identified, no effective solutions can be found.

There is no doubt that some forms of drug use may result in undesirable, unacceptable and anti-social behavior. However, it appears that the overwhelming causes of violent crimes, which often find categorization under the heading of "drug related," are caused by various factors unrelated

> *"Present drug policy appears to contribute to the increase of violence in our communities."*

to actual pharmacological effects of controlled substances upon human behavior. Rather, much of the violent crime can be said to be "drug prohibition-related," insofar as it results from the high costs, huge profits and great stakes involved in the world of drug commerce as is carried on in cities, states and nations throughout the world. Moreover, the complete banning of all forms of use and sale of controlled substances, including marijuana and hashish, has fostered an underworld black market, for both "hard" and "soft" drugs, where violence and weapons possession is part and parcel of doing business under conditions of illegality.

Turf Wars

In cities throughout the United States, we find a proliferation of armed violence resulting from "turf" wars for control of territory for lucrative drug sales, together with regularly recurring dangerous and deadly altercations over drug deals gone bad. In addition to this community-based violence, there are "shoot-outs" between drug dealers and law enforcement officers, the latter developing the need for greater and more powerful weapons, only to be matched and then surpassed by those in the drug trade who have enormous profits, and personal liberty, at stake. The net result of these circumstances has been an extraordinary casualty rate for those involved in the drug trade, injury and death to innocent bystanders "caught in the crossfires," injury and loss of life to law enforcement officers, and a prevailing atmosphere of violence in many inner city communities.

A further byproduct of these conditions is an increase of weapons possession, and thereby, the weapons trade, where use and sale of dangerous and increasingly powerful weapons have proliferated. This widespread possession and use of dangerous and deadly weapons has further resulted in the increase of armed violence in our communities, not always directly related to local drug wars, but fostered

> *"The current form of 'drug prohibition' has generated a great deal of violence, much of it armed violence."*

by the undercurrent of violence, guns and money supported by the drug trade.

We note other ways in which current drug policy is likely serving to exacerbate rather than alleviate violence in our communities. Over the past decades, stepped up law enforcement efforts, disproportionately carried out in our inner city communities, have resulted in large and increasing numbers of minority youth being brought within control of the criminal justice system. It is reported that almost 1 in every 3 young black men in the U.S., between the ages of 20–29, is presently within the control of the criminal justice system—either in prison, on parole or on probation. This figure is up from approximately 1 in every 4 as reported just 5 years ago. Together with the destabilization of families and communities affected by wholesale removal of young men from their ranks, many individuals arrested and incarcerated for the inherently "non-violent" offenses of drug possession or sale, are then exposed to the violence of prison culture. This violence is, in turn, brought back to the communities to which these members invariably return.

Current drug policy's emphasis on drug arrests, prosecution and incarceration, also indirectly increases violence by diverting law enforcement, court and other criminal justice resources from concentration on violent crime and violent criminal offenders. Further, institutional pressures bear upon prosecutors to concentrate on drug case, since the availability of paid and trained police and other law enforcement officers, as primary witnesses in such cases, renders prosecution of drug cases easier and the statistical rates of conviction (or return) more favorable. This is not to discount the political emphasis often placed on prosecution of drug cases, nor, of course, the obligation

> *"In cities throughout the United States, we find a proliferation of armed violence resulting from 'turf' wars for control of territory."*

of prosecutors to process those cases in which legally supportable arrests under current law have been made. The net result has been a dramatic shift in the proportion of "non-violent" to "violent" offenders incarcerated in jails and prisons throughout the United States—such shift decidedly toward imprisonment of "non-violent" drug offenders, further stretching resources and limiting the ability of correctional institutions to hold and maintain "violent" offenders within their walls.

On a more global level, there can be no question that the immense fortunes to be made by involvement in the underground, black market world of drug commerce has resulted in enormous power and wealth for national and international narcotics cartels which, in the experience of various smaller nations, has threatened national security itself.

It is clear, therefore, that the most dangerous threats to our security relating to drugs—in our cities, throughout our nation and even, internationally—derive not from the pharmacological effects of drug usage, but from the violence engaged in and power amassed by an entire industry of underworld figures, driven by the high costs and huge profits to be made in the illicit drug trade.

The Example of Alcohol Prohibition

Searching our nation's history for similar experiences from which we may draw guidance, we turn, as many studying this issue have, to our national experience with alcohol prohibition during the early 20th century. During that era of alcohol prohibition, it was the *illegality* of that "controlled substance," alcohol, which drove up its costs, caused a lucrative black market to develop, and supported a widespread growth in wealth and power for underworld figures and organizations. This, in turn, brought on violence—between competing bootleggers and racketeers, and between these underworld interests and law enforcement officers—as well as other related and unrelated violence, much as we see today with respect to the drug trade, although on a much larger scale. In the case of drugs and "drug prohibition," the illegality of these substances has supported and perpetuated the violent culture and dangerous cartels which have profited from the resulting economic circumstances. As one commentator [Loren Siegel] has remarked:

> "People aren't killing each other because they are high on drugs, any more than
> Al Capone ordered the execution of rival bootleggers because he was drunk."

In the final analysis, it appears evident that our nation's drug policy has not only failed to resolve the problems of violent crime, it has served to exacerbate them. Indeed, our nation's "war on drugs," as it has come to be known, has likely had the net effect of causing a more dangerous "war" to rage within our communities, with the only vision of the future appearing to be, if present trends continue, an increase in violence, the proliferation of weapons, a steady supply of new community based drug dealers, and the continued growth of ever-more dangerous "kingpins" and underworld organizations—all driven by the engine of the lucrative, illegal drug trade.

Non-Penal Models

It follows, therefore, that forms of "decriminalization," "legalization," or ending "drug prohibition," must be seriously considered as alternative directions for future drug strategy, however radical such ideas may presently appear. Accordingly, the Task Force urges the further study of alternative, non-penal based models, in development of future drug policy.

In summary, it is abundantly clear that, whatever the harms presently caused by use and abuse of "controlled" substances in our nation, many of the more pressing concerns with respect to violence in our communities are unlikely to be solved until we find a way to take the profit out of the black market drug trade itself. If we continue to fail in addressing these issues in an objective, rational and progressive manner, we may find ourselves devoured by a larger, more dangerous beast of our own creation.

Drug Policies Should Focus on Harm Reduction

by Ethan Nadelmann

About the author: *Ethan Nadelmann is the director of the Lindesmith Center, a drug-policy research institute in New York City.*

There is a growing drug policy reform movement in the United States. Although few agree upon which aspect of the war on drugs is most disgraceful, or on which alternative to our current policies is most desirable, we do agree on the following: the "war on drugs" has failed to accomplish its stated objectives, and it cannot succeed so long as the U.S. remains a free society; the prohibitionist approach to drug control is responsible for most of the ills commonly associated with America's "drug problem"; and some measure of legal availability and regulation is essential if we are to reduce significantly the negative consequences of both drug use and current drug control policies.

Proponents of the U.S. "war on drugs" focus on one apparent success: the substantial decline during the 1980s in the number of Americans who consume marijuana and cocaine. Yet that decline began well before the federal government launched its "war on drugs" in 1986, and it succeeded principally in reducing illicit drug use among those middle class Americans who were least likely to develop drug-related problems.

Drug War Failures

Far more significant were the dramatic increases in drug and prohibition-related disease, death and crime. Crack cocaine—as much a creature of prohibition as 180 proof moonshine during alcohol Prohibition—became the drug of choice in most inner cities. The scourge of HIV spread rapidly among American drug users, their lovers and children, destroying hundreds of thousands of lives and costing billions of dollars, while government officials studiously ignored evidence that making sterile syringes more readily available to addicts would save lives and dollars. And prohibition-related murder and other violence reached unprecedented levels as a new generation of Al Capones competed for

Excerpted from "The End of the Epoch of Prohibition," by Ethan Nadelmann, in *Cannabis Science: From Prohibition to Human Right,* edited by Lorenz Böllinger. Copyright ©1997 by Peter Lang GmbH. Reprinted with the permission of Peter Lang Publishing.

turf, killing not just one another but innocent bystanders, witnesses and law enforcement officials.

The criminal justice system became bogged down in drug cases. Almost 1.4 million people were arrested for drug law violations in the U.S. in 1994: three-quarters were for simple possession and one-third were for marijuana violations. One-third of felony convictions in state courts were for drug law violations. And about 400,000 people were behind bars for drug law violations in 1995 (out of a total 1.6 million people in prisons and jails), at a cost of around $9 billion per year. A study done for the White House showed that one-third of drug offenders in federal prisons had no history of violent crime and little or no criminal history whatsoever. These prisoners are casualties of a failed policy aimed solely at being "tough on drugs".

> *"Some measure of legal availability and regulation is essential if we are to reduce significantly the negative consequences of . . . current drug control policies."*

Basic Truths

Growing numbers of people have come to acknowledge certain basic truths about drugs and drug policy: first, most people can use most drugs without doing much harm to themselves or anyone else. Only a tiny percentage of the seventy million Americans who have tried marijuana have gone on to have problems with that or any other drug. The same is true for most of the tens of millions of Americans who have used cocaine or hallucinogens. And even most of those who did have a problem at one time or another don't anymore. The fact that a few million Americans have serious problems with illicit drugs today is an issue meriting responsible attention, but it is no reason to demonize those drugs and the people who use them.

The second truth: drugs are here to stay. The time has come for the United States to abandon the tired and foolish rhetoric of a "drug-free society", and to focus instead on learning to live with drugs in such a way that they do the least possible harm to drug users and everyone else. Looking throughout history, one finds few if any civilized societies that did not encounter at least one powerful psychoactive drug. So far as I can ascertain, the societies that proved most successful in minimizing drug-related harms were not those that sought to banish drugs and drug users, but rather those that figured out how to control and manage drug use—through community rituals, initiation rites, the establishment and maintenance of powerful social norms, and so on. It is precisely that challenge that American society now confronts with alcohol: how to live with a very powerful and dangerous drug—more powerful and dangerous than many illicit drugs—whose use we can not effectively prohibit.

The third truth: prohibition is no way to run a drug policy. Americans learned this with alcohol during the first third of this century, and is probably wise enough to stop short of prohibition in its efforts to reduce tobacco use. Prohibitions make sense for kids, and it's reasonable to prohibit drug-related behaviors that pose substantial harms to others, such as driving under the influence of alcohol and other drugs, or smoking in enclosed spaces. It's also a fair compromise when communities acknowledge the right of adults to consume what they desire in private but restrict when and where drugs can be sold and consumed. But the indiscriminate sort of prohibition that now informs U.S. drug policy certainly causes more harm than good. Whatever its benefits in deterring some Americans from becoming drug abusers, drug prohibition is responsible for too much crime, disease and death to qualify as sensible public policy.

Reducing Drug-Related Harm

There's a fourth truth, one that often gets lost in the polarized debate between those, such as Milton Friedman and Thomas Szasz, who favor a fairly free market approach, and those like William Bennett, who favor demonizing drug users and executing drug sellers. Between those extremes lie a plethora of drug policy options, some of which can reduce drug-related crime, disease and death more effectively, and often less expensively, than anything being done now. American drug warriors like to mock the Dutch, pointing to their legalized red light zones, but the fact remains that Dutch drug policy has been dramatically more successful

> *"The time has come for the United States to abandon the tired and foolish rhetoric of a 'drug-free society.'"*

than U.S. drug policy. The average age of their heroin addicts has been increasing for almost a decade, HIV rates among addicts are dramatically lower than in the United States, police focus on major dealers and petty dealers who create public nuisances rather than wasting resources on non-disruptive drug users, and the decriminalized cannabis markets are regulated in a quasi-legal fashion that is far more effective, and inexpensive, than the U.S. approach.

In the Netherlands, as in Switzerland and Australia, and parts of Germany, Austria, Britain, and a growing number of other countries, pragmatism often counts more than moralism in designing drug policies. They officially acknowledge the obvious: that drugs are here to stay and that drug policies need to focus on reducing drug-related harms even among people who can't or won't stop taking drugs. Sterile syringes are readily available, over the counter, from vending machines, or from syringe exchange programs, to prevent the spread of HIV. In the United States, one scientific study after another, culminating in a recent National Academy of Science report commissioned by Congress, has concluded that making sterile syringes available over the counter and through needle exchange programs can save lives and dollars. But politicians still refuse to change the law.

Methadone and Heroin Maintenance

We face similar foolishness when it comes to methadone. Methadone is to street heroin more or less what nicotine chewing gum and skin patches are to cigarettes. Hundreds of studies, as well as a 1996 National Academy of Science report, have concluded that methadone is more effective than any other treatment in reducing heroin-related crime, disease and death. In Australia and much of Europe, addicts who want to reduce or quit their heroin use can obtain a prescription for methadone from a general practitioner and fill the prescription at a local pharmacy. In the United States, by contrast, methadone is the most strictly regulated drug in the pharmacopoeia. It's only available at highly regulated clinics, where clients often receive less than the appropriate dose and are treated more like criminals than patients. There is no good reason for this, just politics, prejudice and ignorance.

Consider one more example: heroin prescription. The Swiss have embarked on a national experiment to determine if they can reduce drug and prohibition-related crime, disease, and death by making pharmaceutical-grade heroin legally available to addicts at regulated clinics. It's now almost two years into the experiment, and the results have been sufficiently encouraging that the experiment has been extended to over a dozen Swiss cities. The Dutch and the Australians now are poised to start their own experiments, and a number of cities in Germany have petitioned their federal government to do likewise.

These programs make sense in part because heroin is safe when prescribed and consumed under sanitary, controlled conditions. Unlike cigarettes and alcohol, it does not destroy human organs. The "high" of heroin, for many experienced consumers, is neither intoxicating like alcohol nor tranquilizing like benzodiazepams. Perhaps the closest analogy is to "smoke-free" cigarettes that deliver a dose of nicotine with fewer associated tars and other carcinogens. Thousands of people have held and/or hold responsible jobs

"Dutch drug policy has been dramatically more successful than U.S. drug policy."

while injecting heroin two or three times per day. This is not, of course, to recommend heroin, but it is to say that there is a world of difference—to both addicts and the rest of us—between "legal" heroin obtained from legal sources and adulterated street heroin purchased at black market prices from criminal entrepreneurs. There are no good scientific or ethical reasons not to try a heroin prescription experiment in the United States—only bad political reasons.

Modest Initiatives

In the 1950s, numerous medical and criminal justice organizations voiced support for heroin maintenance, and many, including the New York Academy of Medicine, proposed restricted programs to provide heroin for "confirmed addicts". The government soundly rejected all maintenance proposals. And in the

1970s, a heroin maintenance project was quashed in New York City under the widespread opposition of conservatives and traditional anti-drug organizations. President Richard Nixon denounced heroin maintenance as a surrender to "weakness and defeat in the drug struggle".

> *"Thousands of people have held and/or hold responsible jobs while injecting heroin two or three times per day."*

One of the standard claims spouted by opponents of drug policy reform is that there's no going back once we reverse course and legalize drugs. But what the reforms in Europe and Australia demonstrate is that the choices are not all or nothing. Virtually all the steps described above represent modest, and relatively low risk, initiatives to reduce drug and prohibition-related harms within the current prohibition regime. At the same time, these steps provide valuable insights for thinking through the consequences of more far reaching drug policy reform.

Undertreatment of Pain

The truth of the matter, however, is that we're unlikely to evolve toward a more effective and humane drug policy unless we, as a society, begin to change the ways we think about drugs and drug control. Consider what may qualify as the most outrageous drug scandal in the United States—the epidemic of undertreatment of pain. Every year, millions of Americans, both adults and children, some terminally ill with cancer, some experiencing severe post-operative pain, others struggling with chronic pain, receive insufficient doses of opiates to treat their pain. In many of those states where a physician can prescribe opiates indefinitely to treat intractable pain, the patient must be reported by the physician to the state as a drug addict. Abundant studies now indicate that the risks of addiction to opiates prescribed for pain relief are slight, and that "addiction" to opiates among the terminally ill is an appropriate course of medical treatment. There are no good medical or other scientific reasons for failing to prescribe adequate doses of opiates to relieve pain—only a pervasive "opiaphobia" that causes doctors to ignore the medical evidence, nurses to turn away from their patients' cries, and patients themselves to prefer debilitating and demoralizing pain to a proper dose of morphine, heroin or Demerol. The origins of this maltreatment are inseparable from those that underlie inhumane policies toward heroin addicts.

Why do a few million Americans persist in using cocaine and heroin despite its illegality? For many, perhaps a majority, it represents a form of self-medication against physical and emotional pain among groups in society that are not so well hooked in to the psychotherapy, Prozac, and other anti-depressants that ease the pain of middle and upper class Americans. Add to that factor one perverse paradox of prohibition: that the market in illicit drugs is so powerful in the inner cities because residents perceive not just a lack of other palliatives for their pain but also few economic opportunities that can compete with the profits of violating prohibition.

The tendency to put anti-drug ideology ahead of the compassionate treatment of pain is apparent in another area as well. Thousands of Americans currently smoke marijuana for purely medical reasons: to ease the nausea of chemotherapy; to reduce the pain of multiple sclerosis and other debilitating diseases; to alleviate the symptoms of glaucoma; to improve appetite among people wasting away from AIDS; and for much else. They use it because it works for them better than any pharmaceutical concoction. Many of these people never smoked marijuana until they discovered its medicinal value. Some are elderly. Some don't particularly care for taking a drug by smoking it; and many don't care for marijuana's psychoactive effects. But virtually all of them are regarded as criminals under the law, and every year many are arrested and jailed. Apart from eight lucky souls who managed to obtain a legal source for their medical prescriptions years ago, everyone else is obliged to obtain their marijuana on the black market. Although more than 75% of Americans believe that marijuana should be available legally for medical purposes, the U.S. federal government refuses to allow legal access or even to sponsor or permit research.

Plenty of Blame

Look within the federal government and it is easy to spread the blame for America's backward drug policies: a cowardly White House unwilling to assume leadership in this area; a Congress so obsessed with looking tough on crime that it's no longer interested in figuring out what makes sense; a former drug czar who debased public debate in this area by equating legalization with genocide; and a drug enforcement/treatment complex so hooked on government dollars that few are willing to speak truth to power. But perhaps the worst offender is the U.S. Drug Enforcement Administration—not the agents who risk their lives trying to apprehend major drug traffickers, but rather the ideologically-driven bureaucrats who intimidate and persecute doctors for prescribing pain medication in medically appropriate (but still legally suspicious) doses, who hobble methadone programs with over-regulation, who acknowledge that law enforcement alone cannot solve the drug problem but then proceed to undermine innovative public health initiatives, who connive against efforts to make marijuana medically

> *"The market in illicit drugs is so powerful in the inner cities because residents perceive . . . few economic opportunities."*

available, and who abuse their power to classify and thereby prohibit psychoactive drugs under federal law. The first step in any real drug policy reform effort at the federal level must be to strip the D.E.A. of the powers it has abused and give them to some other agency—public or private—better able to act in the interests of science, public health, and human rights.

In the past decade, many prominent Americans have spoken out against drug prohibition. Mayor Kurt Schmoke of Baltimore voiced support for legalization in April of 1988. In 1989 both U.S. District Judge Robert Sweet, and former U.S. secretary of state and treasury, George Shultz, endorsed drug law reform, drawing severe criticism from the Bush administration. In 1993, President Clinton's surgeon general, Jocelyn Elders, suggested a government study of legalization, and was fired within months. In September of 1995, Chicago federal appeals court judge Richard Posner, a Reagan administration appointee and leading legal scholar, stated his support for the legalization of marijuana. In April 1996, Juan R. Torruella, chief judge of the Boston Circuit Court of Appeals and the highest ranking Puerto Rican in the federal judiciary, recommended a study of alternatives to prohibition. William Buckley's conservative weekly, *The National Review,* came out in favor of drug legalization in February 1996, with the cover "The War on Drugs Is Lost: Kill It, Go for Legalization, Free Up Police, Courts, Reduce Crime". The famous economist, Milton Friedman, and Executive Director of the American Civil Liberties Union, Ira Glasser, have long supported drug policy reform. And many others have begun to voice their dissatisfaction. Yet the U.S. government refuses to listen or even to discuss the issues. Although Americans are usually loathe to look abroad for solutions to domestic problems, perhaps trends in Europe and Australia will begin to change the debate here.

> *"The first step in any real drug policy reform effort at the federal level must be to strip the D.E.A. of the powers it has abused."*

The Dutch Example Shows That Liberal Drug Laws Can Be Beneficial

by Craig Reinarman

About the author: *Craig Reinarman is a professor of sociology and legal studies at the University of California, Santa Cruz, and the coeditor (with Harry G. Levine) of* Crack in America: Demon Drugs and Social Justice.

In 1972, after an exhaustive study by a team of top experts, President Richard Nixon's hand-picked National Commission on Marijuana and Drug Abuse recommended decriminalization of marijuana. Five years later, President Jimmy Carter and many of his top cabinet officials made the same recommendation to Congress. Both the Commission and the Carter administration felt that the "cure" of imprisonment was worse than the "disease" of marijuana use. U.S. drug control officials argued strenuously that Congress should ignore such recommendations, which it did.

At about the same time, however, the Dutch government's own national commission completed its study of the risks of marijuana. The Dutch Commission also concluded that it made no sense to send people to prison for personal possession and use, so Dutch officials designed a policy that first tolerated and later regulated sales of small amounts of marijuana.

Denouncing the Dutch

Since then, U.S. drug control officials have denounced Dutch drug policy as if it were the devil himself. One former U.S. Drug Czar claimed that all the Dutch youth in Amsterdam's Vondel Park were "stoned zombies." Another said "you can't walk down the street in Amsterdam without tripping over dead junkies." In the Summer of 1998, however, one such slander turned into a small scandal. The first part of this viewpoint examines this incident as a window on the politics of drug policy. The second part offers a more general analysis of

Excerpted from "Why Dutch Policy Threatens the U.S.," by Craig Reinarman, *Het Parool,* July 30, 1998. Revised and reprinted with permission from the author.

why U.S. drug control officials seem to be so threatened by the Dutch example.

In early July 1998, the U.S. Drug Czar, General Barry McCaffrey, announced that he would soon go on a "fact finding tour" of the Netherlands to learn first hand about its drug policy. He quickly made it clear, however, that he would be bringing his own facts. Before he ever left home, McCaffrey denounced the Dutch approach to drugs as "an unmitigated disaster" (*CNN*, July 9, 1998). If he had let it go at that, the General might have avoided international embarrassment for himself and the Clinton administration. But he proceeded to make claims about drugs and crime in the Netherlands that were incorrect and insulting. Dutch officials and journalists immediately caught him with his evidentiary pants down and publicly rebutted his false charges.

False Claims

McCaffrey asserted that drug abuse problems in the Netherlands are "enormous" (Associated Press, July 13, 1998). In fact, the Dutch have no more drug problems than most neighboring countries which do not have "liberal" drug policies. Further, by virtually all measures the Dutch have less drug use and abuse than the U.S.—from a lower rate of marijuana use among teens to a lower rate of heroin addiction among adults.

McCaffrey also claimed, to a room full of journalists, that "The murder rate in Holland is double that in the United States. . . . That's drugs." He cited these figures: 17.58 murders per 100,000 population in the Netherlands, he asserted, vs. 8.22 per 100,000 in the U.S. (Reuters, July 13, 1998). For decades the U.S. has had significantly higher crime rates than other industrialized democracies. This has been reported at least annually by most newspapers and news magazines in the U.S.

Whatever the reason this fact eluded General McCaffrey and his staff, it did not elude the journalists to whom he spoke. In less than 24 hours, the world's media caught and corrected McCaffrey's mistake. They showed that he had arrived at his Dutch figure by lumping homicides together with the much higher number of *attempted* homicides, and that he had *not* done the same for the U.S. figures. Thus, the Drug Czar had compared the U.S. homicide rate with the *com-*

> *"U.S. drug control officials have denounced Dutch drug policy as if it were the devil himself."*

bined rates of homicide and attempted homicide in the Netherlands. The correct Dutch homicide rate, the international press reported, is 1.8 per 100,000 *less than one fourth the U.S. rate* (Centraal Bureau voor de Statistiek, July 13, 1998; Reuters, July 14, 1998). Even this error might have been forgotten if McCaffrey had not gone on to attribute this newfound murderous streak in the Dutch national soul to their drug policy: "That's drugs" he said, apparently unaware that there has never been any evidence that marijuana—the only drug the Dutch ever decriminalized—is a cause of murder.

Then McCaffrey's staff at the Office of National Drug Control Policy dug his agency into a deeper hole. When Dutch Embassy officials confronted Deputy Drug Czar Jim McDonough about the misleading figures, he replied: "Let's say [that's] right. What you're left with is that they [the Dutch] are a much more violent society and more inept [at murder], and that's not

> **"By virtually all measures the Dutch have less drug use and abuse than the U.S."**

much to brag about" (*Washington Times*, July 15, 1998, p. A4). Here, in a stunning blend of ignorance and arrogance, Mr. McDonough compounds his failure to understand the earlier error with an ethnic slur upon the Dutch.

The Dutch Reaction

Dutch officials reacted swiftly to all of this. Joris Vos, Dutch Ambassador to the U.S., publicly released a letter he sent to McCaffrey at the White House:

> I am confounded and dismayed by your description of Dutch drug policy as an unmitigated disaster and by your suggestion that the purpose of that policy is to make it easier for young people. . . . Your remarks . . . have no basis in the facts and figures which your office has at its disposal and which certainly do not originate only from Dutch sources. . . . Apart from the substance, which I cannot agree with, I must say that I find the timing of your remarks—six days before your planned visit to the Netherlands with a view to gaining first-hand knowledge about Dutch drugs policy and its results, rather astonishing. . . . (Reuters, July 14, 1998; *Washington Times*, July 15, 1998, p. A4).

The Foreign Ministry, Justice Ministry, and Health Ministry issued a joint diplomatic press release which can only be called wry understatement:

> The impression had been gained that Mr. McCaffrey was coming to the Netherlands to familiarise himself on the spot with Dutch drugs policy. The Netherlands would not exclude the possibility that if Mr. McCaffrey familiarises himself with the results of Dutch drugs policy, he will bring his views more closely into line with the facts (*Financial Times* [London], July 16, 1998, p. 2).

The reaction in the Dutch press ranged from a kind of ho-hum, 'what else is new' to genuine outrage. I reviewed coverage of the controversy in five Dutch daily newspapers and on two Amsterdam TV news shows. All agreed on the basic facts. All reported that McCaffrey's claims were simply wrong. The only question seemed to be whether he had intended to be insulting. The liberal press seemed to lean a bit more toward the latter interpretation and responded with ridicule. Amsterdam's TV 5, for example, aired a pair of comedians doing brief satirical sketches mimicking a reporter interviewing the U.S. Drug Czar:

Q: "How have you liked your trip so far, General McCaffrey?"

A: "OK, but the weather has been bad; it's been rainy almost every day."

Q: "Why do you suppose that's so, General?"

A: "Drugs."

Q: "What are your impressions of the Netherlands so far, General?"

A: "Very interesting. I look forward to going on to Holland."

Q: "But sir, Holland is the same thing as the Netherlands."

A: "What?! The same country with two names? That's drugs for you."

Even the more conservative newspapers, which are sometimes critical of one or another aspect of Dutch drug policy, took McCaffrey to task. *De Volkskrant,* for example, editorialized that the U.S. Drug Czar "had already lost his war," that his false allegations showed the "bankruptcy of prohibitionism," and that the "American crusade against drugs" had "derailed" (July 15, 1998, p. 1). The Christian Democratic paper, *Trouw,* put the story as their top headline, and quoted a police intelligence source who called the Czar's claims "abuse of statistics" (July 15, 1998, p. 1).

Why Dutch Policy Poses a Threat

The little scandal surrounding McCaffrey's mistakes lasted only a few days in the Dutch press, for they have come to expect this sort of thing from U.S. drug control officials. Dutch citizens of the right and the left, fans and critics of their drug policy, know such claims are false. So do the millions of American tourists who have traveled to the Netherlands. If, as is often said, truth is the first casualty of war, perhaps we should simply expect the same of drug wars.

But such bizarre behavior begs a broader question: Why is a liberal reform in the domestic drug policy of one of the smallest, least powerful nations on earth so threatening to one of the largest and most powerful? U.S. officials are threatened by Dutch drug policy because it cuts directly against the moral ideology underlying U.S. drug policy. And that ideology runs deep in American culture and politics. The U.S. has a history of hysteria about intoxicating substances dating back to the 19th-century Temperance crusade. For over a hundred years, Americans believed that Satan's "demon drink" was the direct cause of poverty, ill health, crime, insanity, and the demise of civilization. This fundamentalist crusade culminated with national alcohol prohibition in 1919.

> *"U.S. officials are threatened by Dutch drug policy because it cuts directly against the moral ideology underlying U.S. drug policy."*

Alcohol Prohibition agents immediately took over the job of creating U.S. drug policy. Without debate, they chose criminalization. A series of drug scares since then has led to the criminalization of more drugs and the imprisonment of more drug users for longer terms. What animated each of these scares, from the crusade against alcohol on, was less public health than the politics of fear—fear of change, fear of foreigners, fear of communists, of

105

the working class, of non-whites, of rebellious college students, and perhaps most centrally, fear of the loss of self control through drinking and drug use.

Creeping Totalitarianism

Having scapegoated drugs for so long, U.S. politicians cannot tolerate a tolerant system like the Dutch. They compete for votes on the basis of whose rhetoric is "tougher" on drugs. The Right-wing Republicans who currently control Congress call President Clinton "soft on drugs" even though more drug users have been imprisoned during his administration than under Reagan and Bush. Clinton appointed McCaffrey Drug Czar not because the General had any training or expertise on drug problems, but because he was a military man who would symbolize "toughness."

"A higher proportion of people have tried marijuana in the U.S. . . . than in the Netherlands where citizens may buy it lawfully."

U.S. drug policy has indeed been getting "tougher." The Czar's budget has increased from $1 billion in 1980 to $17 billion in 1998. The number of drug offenders imprisoned in the U.S. has increased 800% since 1980, mostly poor people of color. This has helped the U.S. achieve the highest imprisonment rate in the industrialized world—550 per 100,000 population, compared to the Netherlands' 79 per 100,000. Under the banner of the war on drugs, a kind of creeping totalitarianism tramples more human rights and civil liberties each year. Tens of millions of citizens—most of whom have never used drugs and all of whom are supposed to be presumed innocent—are subjected to supervised urine tests to get jobs and then to keep jobs. Hundreds of thousands more are searched in their homes or, on the basis of racist "trafficker profiles," on freeways and at airports. Houses, cars, and businesses are seized by the state on the slimmest of suspicions alone. And U.S. school children have been bombarded with more antidrug propaganda than any generation in history.

A Failed War

The actual results of all this suggest why U.S. officials lash out defensively against the Dutch. After more than a decade of deepening drug war, U.S. surveys show that illicit drug use by American youth has increased almost every year since 1991. The U.S. Drug Enforcement Administration admits that hard drugs are just as available, less expensive, and more pure than ever. Hard drug abuse and addiction among the urban poor remain widespread. HIV/AIDS continues to spread most rapidly via injection drug users; meanwhile, the needle exchanges that help stem its spread in every other modern nation remain criminalized in the U.S. A growing number of judges—including several high level federal judges appointed by Republicans—have gone so far as to refuse to apply drug laws that have grown so Draconian they breach all bounds of fairness.

Opinion polls now show a majority of Americans do not believe the war on drugs can be won. More and more are voicing their opposition and seeking alternatives to punitive prohibition. The drug policy reform movement in the U.S. has grown larger and more diverse, attracting support from the American Medical Association, the American Bar Association, the American Public Health Association, the American Society of Criminology, and other professional groups. Not all of these groups support decriminalizing marijuana, but all of them support a shift away from drug war toward the harm-reducing public health approaches pioneered in the Netherlands.

And when such pesky heretics argue that there are alternatives to punitive prohibition, one of their key examples is Dutch drug policy. U.S. drug warriors wish the Netherlands example did not exist, but since they cannot make even small countries disappear, they are reduced to making up their own "facts" about it.

No Disaster

Dutch drug policy is also a threat to drug warriors precisely because it has *not* led to what Czar McCaffrey so confidently called an "unmitigated disaster." Dutch society has its drug problems, of course, but no more and often less than most other modern democracies which have harsher drug laws. Indeed, a higher proportion of people have tried marijuana in the U.S. where millions have been arrested for it than in the Netherlands where citizens may buy it lawfully.

U.S. drug control ideology holds that there is no such thing as *use* of an illicit drug, only abuse. But drug use patterns in the Netherlands show that for the overwhelming majority of users, marijuana is just one more type of *genotsmiddelen* (foods, spices, and intoxicants which give pleasure to the senses) that the Dutch have been importing and culturally domesticating for centuries.

U.S. drug warriors tend to lump all illicit drugs together, as if all were equally dangerous and addictive. Dutch drug policy makes pragmatic distinctions based on relative risks. When U.S. officials are confronted by scientific evidence showing marijuana to be among the least risky drugs, they fall back on the claim that it is a "stepping stone" to hard drugs. But here, too, the evi-

> *"Despite lawful availability, the majority of Dutch people never try marijuana."*

dence from Dutch surveys is heresy: despite lawful availability, the majority of Dutch people never try marijuana, and most who do try it don't continue to use even marijuana very often, much less harder drugs.

In short, the Dutch facts destroy the Drug Czar's core claims. Those who have built their careers in the U.S. drug control complex fear Dutch drug policy like the Catholic Church feared Gallileo: they must believe the Dutch model is a disaster, for if it is not their whole cosmology shatters.

Leaders more secure about the effectiveness and fairness of their own drug policies would feel less need to slander the Dutch approach. Dutch officials do not proselytize, urging other nations to adopt their approach to drug policy, and the U.S. is obviously not obliged to adopt any part of the Dutch model. By the same logic, the U.S. government should realize that other societies do not share its phobias and do not appreciate its tendency toward drug policy imperialism, particularly with U.S. drug abuse rates being what they are.

A Senseless Approach

We inhabit an increasingly multicultural world. A multicultural world is also a multi-lifestyle and multi-morality world. Drug policy, therefore, cannot be as simple as stretch socks—"one size fits all." Neither European integration nor globalized markets erase differences in language, culture, behavior, or politics. Thus, a cookie cutter approach to the world's drug problems, in which each nation's drug policy is identical—whether punitive prohibition or any other model—makes no sense.

The Dutch have a long history of tolerance. Many of the Pilgrims who fled religious persecution in England were sheltered in the Netherlands before they came to America in the early 1600s. The Dutch were brutally conquered by the Nazis in World War II, so they know only too well what absolutist states can do to "deviants" and to individual freedom. Down through the centuries the Dutch have developed a deeply democratic culture which has nurtured non-absolutist approaches to many public problems. In the drug policy arena, they have bravely broadened the range of possibilities to examine, which is as useful for those who want to learn something as it is fearful for those who do not.

Drugs Should Not Be Legalized

by Barry R. McCaffrey

About the author: *Barry R. McCaffrey is the director of the White House Office of National Drug Control Policy (ONDCP), a position that is commonly known as "drug czar."*

Proponents of legalization know that the policy choices they advocate are unacceptable to the American public. Because of this, many advocates of this approach have resorted to concealing their real intentions and seeking to sell the American public legalization by normalizing drugs through a process designed to erode societal disapproval.

For example, ONDCP has expressed reservations about the legalization of hemp as an agricultural product because of the potential for increasing marijuana growth and use. While legitimate hardworking farmers may want to grow the crop to support their families, many of the other proponents of hemp legalization have not been as honest about their goals. A leading hemp activist [Jack Herer] is quoted in the San Francisco Examiner and on the Media Awareness Project's homepage (a group advocating drug policy reforms) as saying he "can't support a movement or law that would lift restrictions from industrial hemp and keep them for marijuana." If legalizing hemp is solely about developing a new crop and not about eroding marijuana restrictions, why does this individual only support hemp deregulation if it is linked to the legalization of marijuana?

Legalization: The Underlying Agenda

Similarly, when Ethan Nadelmann, Director of the Lindesmith Center (a drug research institute), speaks to the mainstream media, he talks mainly about issues of compassion, like medical marijuana and the need to help patients dying of cancer. However, Mr. Nadelmann's own words in other fora reveal his underlying agenda: legalizing drugs. Here is what he advocates:

Personally, when I talk about legalization, I mean three things: the first is to

Excerpted from testimony given by Barry R. McCaffrey before the U.S. House of Representatives, Government Reform and Oversight Committee, and the Subcommittee on Criminal Justice, Drug Policy, and Human Resources, June 16, 1999, Washington, D.C.

make drugs such as marijuana, cocaine, and heroin legal . . . .

I propose a mail order distribution system based on a right of access . . . .

Any good non-prohibitionist drug policy has to contain three central ingredients. First, possession of small amounts of any drug for personal use has to be legal. Second, there have to be legal means by which adults can obtain drugs of certified quality, purity and quantity. These can vary from state to state and town to town, with the Food and Drug Administration playing a supervisory role in controlling quality, providing information and assuring truth in advertising. And third, citizens have to be empowered in their decisions about drugs. Doctors have a role in all this, but let's not give them all the power.

We can begin by testing low potency cocaine products—coca-based chewing gum or lozenges, for example, or products like Mariani's wine and the Coca-Cola of the late 19th century—which by all accounts were as safe as beer and probably not much worse than coffee. If some people want to distill those products into something more potent, let them. . . .

International financier George Soros, who funds the Lindesmith Center, has advocated: "If it were up to me, I would establish a strictly controlled distributor network through which I would make most drugs, excluding the most dangerous ones like crack, legally available." William F. Buckley, Jr. has also called for the "legalization of the sale of most drugs, except to minors."

> **"Harm reduction is too often a linguistic ploy to confuse the public."**

Similarly, when the legalization community explains their theory of harm reduction—the belief that illegal drug use cannot be controlled and, instead, that government should focus on reducing drug-related harms, such as overdoses—the underlying goal of legalization is still present. For example, in a 1998 article in *Foreign Affairs*, Mr. Nadelmann expressed that the following were legitimate "harm reduction" policies: allowing doctors to prescribe heroin for addicts; employing drug analysis units at large dance parties, known as raves, to test the quality of drugs; and "decriminalizing" possession and retail sale of cannabis and, in some cases, possession of "hard drugs."

Legalization, whether it goes by the name harm reduction or some other trumped up moniker, is still legalization. For those who at heart believe in legalization, harm reduction is too often a linguistic ploy to confuse the public, cover their intentions and thereby quell legitimate public inquiry and debate. Changing the name of the plan doesn't constitute a new solution or alter the nature of the problem. . . .

Fallacies and Realities of Drug Legalization

FALLACY: Drug legalization will not increase drug use.

REALITY: Drug legalization would significantly increase the human and economic costs associated with drugs.

Proponents argue that legalization is a cure-all for our nation's drug problem. However, the facts show that legalization is not a panacea but a poison. In reality, legalization would dramatically expand America's drug dependence, significantly increase the social costs of drug abuse, and put countless more innocent lives at risk. . . .

During the 1970s, our nation engaged in a serious debate over the shape of our drug control policies. (For example, within the context of this debate, between 1973 and 1979, eleven states "decriminalized" mari-

> *"The United States has tried drug legalization and rejected it several times now because of the suffering it brings."*

juana). During this timeframe, the number of Americans supporting marijuana legalization hit a modern-day high. While it is difficult to show causal links, it is clear that during this same period, from 1972 to 1979, marijuana use rose from 14 percent to 31 percent among adolescents, 48 percent to 68 percent among young adults, and 7 percent to 20 percent among adults over twenty-six. This period marked one of the largest drug use escalations in American history.

A similar dynamic played out nationally in the late 1800s and early 1900s. Until the 1890s, today's controlled substances—such as marijuana, opium, and cocaine—were almost completely unregulated. It was not until the last decades of the 1800s that several states passed narcotics control laws. Federal regulation of narcotics did not come into play until the Harrison Act of 1914.

Prior to the enactment of these laws, narcotics were legal and widely available across the United States. In fact, narcotics use and its impacts were commonplace in American society. Cocaine was found not only in early Coca-Cola (until 1903) but also in wine, cigarettes, liqueur-like alcohols, hypodermic needles, ointments, and sprays. Cocaine was falsely marketed as a cure for hay fever, sinusitis and even opium and alcohol abuse. Opium abuse was also widespread. One year before Bayer introduced aspirin to the market, the company also began marketing heroin as a "nonaddictive," no prescription necessary, over-the-counter cure-all.

A Well Worn, Dead-End Path

During this period, drug use and addiction increased sharply. While there are no comprehensive studies of drug abuse for this period that are on par with our current *National Household Survey on Drug Abuse and Monitoring the Future* studies, we can, for example, extrapolate increases in opium use from opium imports, which were tracked. Yale University's Dr. David Musto, one of the leading experts on the patterns of drug use in the United States, writes: "The numbers of those overusing opiates must have increased during the nineteenth century as the per capita importation of crude opium increased from less than 12 grains annually in the 1840s to more than 52 grains in the 1890s." Only in the 1890s when societal concerns over and disapproval of drug use began to become widespread and triggered legal responses did these rates level off. Until this change in attitudes began to denormalize drug use, the United States experienced over a 400 percent increase in opium use alone. This jump is even more staggering if one considers that during this period other serious drugs, such as cocaine, were also widely available in every-day products.

Moreover, while we do not believe that the period of prohibition on alcohol is directly analogous to current efforts against drugs, our experiences with alcohol prohibition also raise parallel concerns. While prohibition was not without its flaws, during this period alcohol usage fell to between 30 to 50 percent of its pre-prohibition levels. From 1916 to 1919 (just prior to when prohibition went into effect in 1920), U.S. alcohol consumption averaged 1.96 gallons per person per year. During prohibition, alcohol use fell to a low of .90 gallons per person per year. In the decade that followed prohibition's repeal, alcohol use increased to a per capita annual average of 1.54 gallons and has since steadily risen to 2.43 gallons in 1989. Prohibition also substantially reduced the rates of alcohol-related illnesses.

The United States has tried drug legalization and rejected it several times now because of the suffering it brings. The philosopher Santayana was right in his admonition that "those who cannot remember the past are condemned to repeat it." Let us not now be so foolish as to once again consider this well worn, dead-end path.

The Impact on Youth

Most importantly the legalization of drugs in the United States would lead to a disproportionate increase in drug use among young people. In 1975, the Alaskan Supreme Court invalidated certain sections of the state's criminal code pertaining to the possession of marijuana. Based on this finding, from 1975 to 1991, possession of up to four ounces of the drug by an adult who was lawfully in the state of Alaska became legal. Even though marijuana remained illegal for children, marijuana use rates among Alaskan youth increased significantly. In response, concerned Alaskans, in particular the National Federation of Parents for Drug-Free Youth, sponsored an anti-drug referendum that was approved by the voters in 1990, once again rendering marijuana illegal.

> *"Legalization would send a strong message that taking drugs is a safe and socially accepted behavior."*

In addition to the impact of expanded availability, legalization would have a devastating effect on how our children see drug use. Youth drug use is driven by attitudes. When young people perceive drugs as risky and socially unacceptable youth drug use drops. Conversely, when children perceive less risk and greater acceptability in using drugs, their use increases. If nothing else, legalization would send a strong message that taking drugs is a safe and socially accepted behavior that is to be tolerated among our peers, loved ones and children. Such a normalization would play a major role in softening youth attitudes and, ultimately, increasing drug use.

The significant increases in youth drug use that would accompany legalization are particularly troubling because their effects would be felt over the course of a generation or longer. Without help, addictions last a lifetime. Every additional young person we allow to become addicted to drugs will impose tremendous human and fiscal burdens on our society. Legalization would be a usurious debt upon our society's future—the costs of such an approach would mount exponentially with each new addict, and over each new day.

> *"If drugs were legalized, the United States would see significant increases in the number of drug users."*

The Impact of Drug Prices

If drugs were legalized, we can also expect that the attendant drop in drug prices to cause drug use rates to grow as drugs become increasingly affordable to buy. Currently a gram of cocaine sells for between $150 and $200 on U.S. streets. The cost of cocaine production is as low as $3 per gram. In order to justify legalization, the market cost for legalized cocaine would have to be set so low as to make the black market, or bootleg cocaine, economically unappealing. Assume, for argument sake, that the market price was set at $10 per gram, a three hundred percent plus markup over cost, each of the fifty hits of cocaine in that gram could retail for as little as ten cents.

With the cost of "getting high" as low as a dime (ten cents)—about the cost of a cigarette—the price of admission to drug use would be no obstacle to anyone even considering it. However, each of these "dime" users risks a life-long drug dependence problem that will cost them, their families, and our society tens of thousands of dollars.

In addition to the impact on youth, we would also expect to see falling drug prices drive increasing drug use among the less affluent. Among these individuals the price of drug use—even at today's levels—remains a barrier to entry into use and addiction. The impact of growing use within these populations could be severe. Many of these communities are already suffering the harms of drug use—children who see no other future turning to drugs as an escape, drug dealers driving what remains of legitimate business out of their communities, and families being shattered by a loved one hooked on drugs. Increased drug use would set back years of individual, local, state and federal efforts to sweep these areas clean of drugs and build new opportunities.

FALLACY: Drug legalization would reduce the harm of drug use on our society.

REALITY: Drug legalization would cost billions of dollars and risk millions of additional innocent lives.

By increasing the rates of drug abuse, legalization would exact a tremendous cost on our society. If drugs were legalized, the United States would see significant increases in the number of drug users, the number of drug addicts, and the number of people dying from drug-related causes.

While many of these costs would fall first and foremost on the user, countless other people would also suffer if drugs were legalized. Contrary to what libertarians and legalizers would have us believe, drug use is not a victimless crime.

Increases in Child Abuse and Neglect

Innocent children suffer the most from drug abuse. In *No Safe Havens*, experts from Columbia University's Center for Addiction and Substance Abuse found that substance abuse (including drugs and alcohol) exacerbates seven of every ten child abuse or neglect cases. In the last ten years, driven by substance abuse, the number of abused and neglected children has more than doubled, up from 1.4 million in 1986 to three million in 1997. In 1994, the *American Journal of Public Health* reported that children whose parents abuse drugs or alcohol are four times more likely to be neglected and/or abused than children with parents who were not drug abusing.

> *"Children whose parents abuse drugs or alcohol are four times more likely to be neglected and/or abused."*

If drugs were made legal, among the growing ranks of the addicted will be scores of people with children. Given the clear linkage between rates of addiction and child abuse and neglect, more drug use will cause tens of thousands of additional children to suffer from abuse and neglect as parents turn away from their children to chase their habit.

Increases in Drugged Driving Accidents

Over the last ten years, Americans have grown increasingly aware of the death toll related to drinking and driving. While we focus less on the risks of drugged driving, the fact is that if the driver on the road next to you is drugged, you and whoever is riding with you are at risk. A National Transportation Safety Board study of 182 fatal truck accidents revealed that 12.5 percent of the drivers had used marijuana, in comparison to 12.5 percent who used alcohol, 8.5 percent who used cocaine and 7.9 percent who used stimulants. Illegal drugs (marijuana, cocaine, and stimulants combined) were present in more accidents than alcohol—even though alcohol is legal and far more available. "A study of 440 drivers, ages 15 to 34 years old, who were killed in California during a two-year period detected alcohol and marijuana in one-third of victims. More than one-half consumed a drug or drugs other than alcohol," according to the NTSB.

Historically, we believe that impaired drivers drive more recklessly. A 1995 roadside study conducted in Memphis, Tennessee of reckless drivers not believed to be impaired by alcohol, found that 45 percent tested positive for marijuana.

Drugged Driving Among Young People

Most disturbingly, drugged driving often appears among the most inexperienced drivers, namely young people. The *1996 National Household Survey on Drug Abuse* found that 13 percent of young people aged sixteen to twenty drove a car less than two hours after drug use at least once during the past year. These young drivers are generally unaware of the dangers they present to themselves and others. Among 16 to 20 year olds who drove after marijuana use, 57 percent said they did so because they were not "high enough to cause a crash." When a person using drugs takes the wheel, his drug use is likely to have human costs. Not only is the drugged driver at risk, but all those around him are as well. On January 29, 1999, a car with five young girls—high school juniors in a middle class suburb of Philadelphia—crashed into a tree, killing the driver and the other occupants. The medical examiner's report concluded that the driver lost control of the car not because of speed or inexperience but because she was impaired from "huffing"—inhaling a chemical solvent—to get high. Three of the passengers were also found to have used the drug. Five more young people, all with bright futures, are dead because of drug use behind the wheel.

> *"If drugs were legalized the rate of drugged driving would increase."*

If drugs were legalized the rate of drugged driving would increase. Added to the countless tragedies caused by drinking and driving would be scores of deaths and injuries from people taking legalized drugs and driving while impaired.

According to the National Highway Traffic Safety Administration (NHTSA), there were 16,189 alcohol-related traffic fatalities in 1997 (38.6 percent of the total traffic fatalities for the year). NHTSA also reports that in 1997, more than 327,000 people were injured in auto crashes where police reported that alcohol was present. These tragic statistics make abundantly clear the risks we would face if other drugs, such as heroin, marijuana and LSD, were made legal and widely available.

Increases in Workplace Accidents, Decreasing Productivity

Just as drug impairment behind the wheel puts others at risk, so too does impairment on the job. Since over 60 percent of drug users in the United States are employed, it is not surprising that workplace drug use is a significant problem. According to a 1995 Gallup survey, 35 percent of American employees report having seen drug use on the job by co-workers. One-in-ten report having been offered drugs while at work. Drug use in the workplace diminishes productivity and increases costs. Drug using employees are more likely to have taken an unexcused absence in the last month, and are more likely to change or leave a job. The National Institute on Drug Abuse and the National Institute on Alcohol Abuse and Alcoholism estimated that the cost to our nation's productivity from illegal drug use was $69.4 billion in 1992. Increasing rates of drug use burden our economy as a whole. They also place businesses, in particular small businesses, at risk. In the end, it is the American consumer who ultimately pays these costs.

When drugs are mixed with the heavy machinery of industry, the results can be devastating. In 1987, a Conrail freight train operated by an engineer who had been smoking marijuana struck an Amtrak passenger train, killing sixteen people and injuring more than one hundred. In July 1998, a passenger train and a truck carrying steel coils collided. The driver of the truck, who was cited by police for more than a dozen violations relating to the crash, tested positive for marijuana immediately following the accident. The collision dislodged one of the twenty-ton coils, causing it to roll through the train's first passenger compartment, killing three and injuring others.

Highly publicized disasters like these capture the public's attention. However, the harms of drug abuse build incrementally on job sites all across the nation every day. Utah Power & Light employees who tested positive on pre-employment drug tests were five times more likely to be involved in a workplace accident than those who tested negative. The 1995 Gallup survey similarly found that 42 percent of American employees believe that drug use greatly affects workplace safety. Even these numbers are likely to underestimate the harms caused by drugs on the job; for a variety of reasons drug-related on-the-job injuries are likely under-reported.

Measuring On-the-Job Injuries

One way to factor the risks presented by on-the-job drug use is to extrapolate from the rate at which drug-free workplace programs can reduce job-related accidents. For example, the Boeing corporation's drug-free workplace program has saved over $2 million in employee medical claims. At Southern Pacific railroad, the injury rate dropped 71 percent with the development of a drug-free workplace assistance program. One of the major auto manufacturers has reported 82 percent decline in job-related accidents since implementing an employee substance abuse assistance program. Similarly, an Ohio study found that substance abuse treatment programs significantly reduced on-the-job injuries. If job-related drug assistance programs can prevent such high rates of accidents, it follows that drugs cause large numbers of injuries among America's employees.

"If drugs were made legal, use—including on-the-job drug use—will increase."

If drugs were made legal, use—including on-the-job drug use—will increase.

Growing numbers of drug users operating heavy equipment, driving tractor-trailers, and operating buses, would inevitably lead to greater numbers of workplace injuries. While the impaired drug user is most at risk from their own actions, countless innocent people—co-workers and ordinary citizens—would also face added dangers. Additionally, apart from the human costs, significantly increased numbers of on-the-job drug-related accidents would cost the American economy countless millions—ranging from rising insurance costs, to personal injury settlements, to losses through decreased productivity.

Flawed Logic

FALLACY: Drugs are harmful because they are illegal.

REALITY: Drugs are harmful not because they are illegal; they are illegal because they are harmful.

Critics argue that the harm to our society from drugs, such as the costs of crime, could be reduced if drugs were legalized. The logic is flawed. By increasing the availability of drugs, legalization would dramatically increase the harm to innocent people. With more drugs and drug use in our society, there would be more drug-related child abuse, more drugged driving fatalities, and more drug-related workplace accidents. None of these harms are caused by law or law enforcement but by illegal drugs.

Even with respect to the crime-re-

> *"Even if drugs were legal, people would still steal and prostitute themselves to pay for addictive drugs."*

lated impact of drugs, drug-related crimes are driven far more by addiction than by the illegality of drugs. Law enforcement doesn't cause people to steal to support their habits; they steal because they need money to fuel an addiction—a drug habit that often precludes them from earning an honest living. Even if drugs were legal, people would still steal and prostitute themselves to pay for addictive drugs and support their addicted lifestyles. Dealers don't deal to children because the law makes it illegal; dealers deal to kids to build their market by hooking them on a life-long habit at an early age, when drugs can be marketed as cool and appealing to young people who have not matured enough to consider the real risks. Make no mistake: legalizing drugs won't stop pushers from selling heroin and other drugs to kids. Legalization will, however, increase drug availability and normalize drug-taking behavior, which will increase the rates of youth drug abuse.

For example, although the Dutch have adopted a more tolerant approach to illegal drugs, crime is in many cases increasing rapidly in Holland. The most recent international police data (1995) shows that Dutch per capita rates for breaking and entering, a crime closely associated with drug abuse, are three times the rate of those in Switzerland and the United States, four times the French rate, and 50 percent greater than the German rate. "A 1997 report on hard-drug use in the

Netherlands by the government-financed Trimbos Institute acknowledged that 'drug use is considered the primary motivation behind crimes against property'—23 years after the Dutch [drug] policy was supposed to put a brake on that," Larry Collins reports. Moreover, *Foreign Affairs* recently noted that in areas of Holland where youth cannabis smokers are most prevalent, such as Amsterdam, Utrecht and Rotterdam, the rates of juvenile crime have "witnessed skyrocketing growth" over the last three to four years. Statistics from the Dutch Central Bureau of Statistics indicate that between 1978 and 1992, there was a gradual, steady increase in violence of more than 160 percent.

"America's criminal justice system is not the root cause of drug-related crime."

In contrast, crime rates in the United States are rapidly dropping. For example, the rate of drug-related murders in the United States has hit a ten-year low. In 1989, there were 1,402 drug-related murders. By 1997 that number fell to 786. In 1995, there were 581,000 robberies in the United States. By 1997, that number fell to roughly 498,000.

America's criminal justice system is not the root cause of drug-related crime. It is the producers, traffickers, pushers, gangs and enforcers who are to blame, as are all the people who use drugs and never think about the web of criminality and suffering their drug money supports.

The Public Should Oppose Drug Legalization

by A.M. Rosenthal

About the author: *A.M. Rosenthal is a columnist for the* New York Times.

"It's nice to think that in another five or ten years maybe the right over one's consciousness, the right to possess and consume drugs, may be as powerfully and as widely understood as the other rights of Americans are."

If that thought strikes you too as nice, you don't have to do much. Just lean back and enjoy the successes of Dr. Ethan Nadelmann, who said it in 1993, and other executives of well-financed "drug reform" foundations.

Maybe he is a little optimistic about his timing. But he and others who would like now-illegal drugs to be a right certainly have made political headway since his pronouncement at the San Francisco conference to celebrate the 50th anniversary of the discovery of LSD.

A Horrible Thought

Still, perhaps the thought that narcotics will become a basic American right strikes you as plain horrible. Perhaps you have love for your children, or theirs, or for the mental, moral and civil stability of the country in which you live.

Perhaps you will become worried about a new report from the Partnership for a Drug-Free America. It shows that marijuana use among children and teen-agers is increasing, and parents don't know it, and that children and teen-agers find it much easier to get, and parents don't know it, and that among the youngsters the fear of the risks of the drug is decreasing—and parents don't know that either.

Or, maybe you will be startled at the report's finding that parents think they talk to their children about drugs a lot more than their children recall hearing—and wonder if the parents remember right.

Or it could be that you are sick to the gorge of the press and TV accepting the flood of false compassion that reformers used to attain the triumph of "medicalization" of marijuana in California and Arizona. Perhaps you know the "reformers," supported by benefactors like George Soros, Peter Lewis of Ohio and John Sperling of Arizona, plan to use the same weapon in other referendums across the country.

Get Up and Fight

Then, under any of those conditions, the time has come for you to get up and fight against drugs, instead of just looking worried. Here are three ways:

1. With your votes, letters, mouths and religious and social organizations, pressure the people you elect to every level of government. Demand detailed exposure of backdoor legalization, its funders and techniques.

Ask the President, again and again and again, to become the political, passionate leader against drugs that the country lacks and so terribly needs. Maybe he will never do it, which does not excuse us from saying it is his duty.

2. Join and support organizations that actively fight drugs and ask that Congress fully restore the funds it cut from their anti-drug education work. Pester newspapers and TV to give full hearings to the organizations and to the anti-drug case. And if the organizations are not on the Internet, tell them they are surrendering to the crowds of legalizers who are.

(National Families in Action, an anti-drug organization, publishes "A Guide to the Drug Legalization Movement and How to Fight It," a most useful book in which I came across Dr. Nadelmann's "nice" thought. www.emory.edu/NFIA).

3. Any way you can, spread the truth that law enforcement, drug interdiction and therapy are all necessary to fight the war, and that therapy, especially in prisons, is not getting enough government funds. Help therapeutic communities like Phoenix House, Daytop Village and others.

Expect no medals. Many journalists have used drugs, particularly marijuana, and having survived themselves think everybody can. And America's best-known writers are either cold to the drug war or apparently never heard of it. American pop stars would rather go bald than fight narcotics.

> *"Parents think they talk to their children about drugs a lot more than their children recall hearing."*

But 87 percent of Americans are against legalization, which is why legalizers use euphemisms and back doors and have to depend on big donors, not little ones.

If you help the huge anti-drug majority know its strengths and the backdoor techniques of the legalizers, then parents and their children will not only talk at home about drugs, but hear each other.

Drug Legalization Would Lead to Increased Drug Abuse

by Thomas A. Constantine

About the author: *Thomas A. Constantine is the former superintendent of the New York State Police and the former administrator of the Drug Enforcement Administration (DEA).*

During my 39-year career in law enforcement, in my positions as Superintendent of the New York State Police and as Administrator of the Drug Enforcement Administration, and now as I return to private life, I have passionately believed that legalizing drugs is wrong, immoral, and suicidal for our society. Having seen first-hand the devastation that drug use and availability have had on many segments of our society over the past thirty years, I know deep in my heart that any effort to make more drugs available to the American people including our children and the poor—which, make no mistake is what legalization advocates are suggesting—will have devastating consequences for our entire nation.

When I look at just who is proposing drug legalization I am struck by several things, including the fact that they are mostly affluent, well-educated and socially distant from the potential victims of their experiment. The legalization movement is well-financed and has been spawned in salons in the Upper East side of New York, country clubs on both coasts of the nation, and in locations remote from the realities of drug addiction, despair and the social decay that accompany drug use. The people who are missing from the legalization debate, and this is no accident, are mothers, religious leaders, and the loved ones of those who have been victimized by crime and addiction. Law enforcement officials are also absent from the ranks of those who are calling for legalization, not because we have a vested interest in enforcing the drug laws of the United States, but because we have seen how dangerous and divesting drug use and traf-

Excerpted from testimony given by Thomas A. Constantine before the U.S. House of Representatives, Government Reform and Oversight Committee, Subcommittee on Criminal Justice, Drug Policy, and Human Resources, July 13, 1999.

ficking have been, particularly in poorer urban and rural areas of our country. . . .

Many legalization advocates claim that drugs should be legalized in order to satisfy what they characterize as "America's insatiable demand for drugs." From my experience, and the experience of the vast majority of law enforcement officials, it is clear that drug availability leads to increased drug use.

At the current time, American communities are being targeted by powerful international drug trafficking organizations based overseas with headquarters in Colombia and Mexico. These organizations are responsible for sending all of the cocaine, and the majority of the marijuana, heroin, and methamphetamine available in U.S. communities. Beginning in the 1970s, when Colombia-based trafficking organizations eclipsed American organized crime groups as the preeminent force in drug trafficking, drug users in the United States were supplied with marijuana, and then cocaine from groups based in Medellin and Cali. We know now, as we suspected then, that the goal of these ruthless organizations was to flood the United States with their poisonous drugs. They saturated U.S. cities with multi-ton quantities of cocaine and created an unprecedented demand. This was a clear case of supply driving demand.

I'd like to go right to the heart of this debate and address an issue that we could spend countless hours discussing: how does supply influence demand? I have always believed that supply not only influences, but *creates* demand. It is not only the quantity of cocaine or heroin that influences usage, but more importantly, the available supply.

Marketing Heroin

Let me give you an example. A few years back, Colombian traffickers decided to diversify into the heroin market and made a strategic marketing decision to push heroin as an alternative to cocaine. They were, unfortunately, very successful, and today, 75 percent of heroin sold in the United States is smuggled in from South America. Their savvy marketing techniques included the bundling of heroin along with cocaine and providing "free samples" to hawk to potential buyers. Also, brand names of heroin were created and certain dealers only provided those brands to instill customer loyalty and brand-name recognition. Ultimately, they created a stronger, cheaper, and more appealing product. Purity levels increased from single digits to today's heroin that ranges from 40 to 90 percent pure. As a result, it can be snorted and smoked, rather than injected, thus enticing a whole new generation of users who would otherwise be turned off by needles.

> *"Any effort to make more drugs available to the American people . . . will have devastating consequences."*

As a result of this combination of higher purity, lower prices, and ready availability in open drug markets, the United States is experiencing a dramatic increase in heroin abuse. Today's heroin mortality figures are the highest ever recorded, exceeding even those of the mid 1970s, when deaths reached a high point just over 2,000. Close to over 4,000 people died in the last three years from heroin-related overdoses. Heroin abuse has taken a toll on a wide range of American communities such as Baltimore and Orlando in the East and suburban cities such as Plano, Texas, in the west.

The Reemergence of Methamphetamine

The fact that drug supply leads to increased drug demand is also being demonstrated by the skyrocketing up-surge in methamphetamine abuse in our country. Methamphetamine, which had appealed to a relatively small number of American users, has reemerged as a major drug of choice.

Historically controlled by outlaw motorcycle gangs, methamphetamine production and trafficking is now controlled by sophisticated organized crime drug groups from Mexico, operating in that country and in California. These groups systematically increased both the production and distribution of methamphetamine, and as a result, statistics illustrate that methamphetamine use and availability has dramatically increased to epidemic proportions throughout the United States in a short period of time. The Drug Abuse Warning Network (DAWN) indicates that emergency room episodes involving methamphetamine increased from 4,900 in 1991 to 17,400 in 1997, an increase of 280%. The areas hardest hit by the methamphetamine epidemic are Dallas, Denver, Los Angeles, Minneapolis, Phoenix, San Diego, San Francisco, and Seattle.

*"Supply not only influences, but **creates demand**."*

Methamphetamine trafficking and abuse are spreading across the United States at an alarming rate. With their primary methamphetamine production headquartered in remote areas of California, the surrogates of Mexican organized crime groups are also establishing a presence in cities in the Midwest, the deep South and the East Coast. Barely heard of a decade before in the nation's heartland, methamphetamine has taken hold of Des Moines, Iowa, and many other Midwestern cities. Trafficking gangs from Mexico introduced this highly addictive stimulant to citizens there, and the problem has become so significant that meth has been cited as a contributing factor in an estimated 80 percent of the domestic violence cases in Iowa.

By these examples, I do not mean to imply in the least that demand is not a critical factor in the equation. I want to stress, however, that supply definitely generates increased drug use. America's two current drug epidemics—heroin and methamphetamine—support this thesis. Legalization would only make a bad situation more dangerous.

I believe that the application of aggressive law enforcement principles and techniques, rather than drug legalization/decriminalization, is the most successful way to dismantle international drug trafficking organizations and reduce the number of drug users in this country. America's drug enforcement policies are working: from 1979 to 1994, the number of drug users in America dropped by almost half.

Aggressive law enforcement has also reduced the levels of violent crime so often associated with drug abuse and drug trafficking. Within the last several years, it has become very clear that the recent reductions in the violent crime rate within the United States in places like New York, Los Angeles and Houston—now at levels not seen since the 1960s—are due in large part to aggressive law enforcement at all levels. The New York City example is perhaps the most compelling illustration of this point. In the early 1990s after three decades of rapidly increasing levels of violent crime which were exacerbated by the crack epidemic, the City of New York embarked upon an ambitious program to enhance its law enforcement capabilities. City leaders increased the police department by 30%, adding 8,000 officers. Arrests for all crimes, including drug dealing, drug gang activity, and quality of life violations which had been tolerated for many years, increased by 50%. The capacity of New York prisons was also increased. The results of these actions were dramatic: the total number of homicides in 1998—633—was less than the number of murders in 1964. Over an eight-year period the number of homicides was reduced from 2262 to 633—a reduction of more than 70%.

> *"Legalization would only make a bad situation more dangerous."*

DEA has also been aggressive in developing and implementing programs to reduce violent narcotics-related crime. One enforcement program, the Mobile Enforcement Teams, lends support to local and state law enforcement agencies that are experiencing problems arising from violent drug-related crime in their communities. The results of this program over the past four years indicate that aggressive law enforcement of drug laws does have a lasting impact on reducing crime and improving the quality of life for the residents of communities across the nation. Statistics indicate that on average, communities participating in the MET program have seen a 12% reduction in homicides. But just as important to me have been the scores of letters the DEA has received from leaders in these communities recognizing this decrease in crime and thanking us for helping achieve a more peaceful way of life for citizens.

Drug abuse, along with the combination of violent crime and social decay that accompany it, can be prevented. Too many people in America seem resigned to the inevitability of rampant drug use. However, effective law enforcement programs make a difference, and we must stay the course.

The Reality of Legalization

Legalization proponents are telling Americans that drugs are not dangerous, that increased addiction is not a significant threat to America, and that inner cities will be better off because it is drug dealing—not drug use—that is the problem.

The legalization advocates are not telling the truth about the consequences of their proposal. It is not that they are purposely misleading Americans, but rather they are not providing all of the information necessary for us to make a sound judgment on the issue. The logistics of legalizing drugs are overwhelming. Take pharmaceuticals for example. Despite tough regulations and strict controls, these powerful and addicting legalized drugs remain the most widely abused drugs in the country. Surely the same would happen with legalized heroin, cocaine, and methamphetamine.

Unanswered Questions

There are many tough questions to ask legalization advocates. I believe many cannot be answered adequately. Some of these include:

Will all drugs be legalized? Will we knowingly make dangerous, mind-altering, addictive substances—PCP, LSD, crack, methamphetamine—available to everyone—regardless of their health? profession? age? past criminal record?

How do we address the black market that will inevitably spring up to provide newer, purer, more potent drugs to those now addicted who cannot be satisfied with the product they obtain from the government or the private sector?

Given the fact that our record with cigarettes and alcohol is not very good, how will we limit the abundance of dangerous drugs to 18 or 21 year olds?

> *"Aggressive law enforcement of drug laws does have a lasting impact on reducing crime and improving the quality of life."*

Who will pay for the health costs and social costs which will accrue as a result of increased drug use? Who will pay for the losses in productivity and absenteeism ?

Whose taxes will pay for the thousands of babies born drug-addicted?

What responsibility will our society have to these children as they grow and have problems as a result of their drug use?

Will drug centers be located in the inner cities, or will drug distribution centers be set up in the suburbs?

And most legalization experts cannot answer this question: Can we set up a legalization pilot program in your neighborhood?

No Surrender

These are all questions we should ask and answers we should demand. Granted, we have not yet effectively addressed all of the drug problems facing our nation today, but we must also realize that the drug issue is a very complex problem that has been with us for decades. It will take more time for us to see our way clear.

Despite this realization, it is astounding to me that legalization proponents advocate surrender. Our nation is faced with other major problems besides drug use: AIDS, declining educational standards, homelessness—yet we do not hear cries for us to abandon our efforts and surrender to inaction on these issues. Why is the drug issue different?

> *"Ask yourself if we in fact would be better off as a society freely dispensing drugs to anyone who wanted them."*

We do not advocate giving up on our schools, or negating everything we've done to date to find a cure for cancer—even though we have spent billions of dollars on research and we have not yet found a cure.

In closing, I ask each of you to think about these questions, and to ask yourself if we in fact would be better off as a society freely dispensing drugs to anyone who wanted them. Given the enormous challenges our nation faces in the years ahead, I cannot honestly envision a world where our surgeons, pilots, or children are given license by our government—which has an obligation to protect and defend all of us—to take dangerous and addictive drugs.

Drug Policies Should Not Be Based on the Harm Reduction Model

by Herbert D. Kleber and Mitchell S. Rosenthal

About the authors: *Herbert D. Kleber is executive vice president and medical director at the National Center on Addiction and Substance Abuse and director of the Division on Substance Abuse Research at Columbia University's College of Physicians and Surgeons. Mitchell S. Rosenthal is president of Phoenix House, a national network of drug treatment and prevention facilities.*

Few issues generate more heat than substance abuse. Most Americans yearn for simple solutions that will make the problem go away. Ethan A. Nadelmann thinks he has found some in the experiences of some foreign countries. These, he argues, are sensible alternatives to America's failed policies ("Commonsense Drug Policy," *Foreign Affairs*, January/February 1998). But his analysis merely further disseminates myths about overseas "successes" that do much to hinder the evolution of reasonable, popular, and effective U.S. drug policies.

Nadelmann maintains that "drugs are here to stay" and focuses on reducing the harm they cause. True, the United States will never be totally drug-free, any more than it will ever be totally crime-free or disease-free. But that is no cause for despair. Were the United States committed to an unambiguous and full-scale confrontation with illicit drugs, drug use could be brought down to a bare minimum and its extraordinary social and economic costs substantially reduced. There is no convincing evidence that liberalizing drug policies and accommodating drug use will reduce these harmful effects. Nor is there evidence of a need to ease up now. There is, however, ample proof that the consistent exercise of restrictive policies can minimize the damage. Such policies brought drug abuse under control in societies as diverse as Japan and Sweden. Widespread drug use need not be a fixture of modern life.

The Swiss Experience

Those who advocate abandoning U.S. efforts to contain drug abuse often urge Americans to learn from the experiences of other countries. One of their favorite "successes" is Switzerland, which Nadelmann lauds for supposedly showing that keeping addicts on heroin prevents them from committing crimes and using other drugs. Organizers of a 1994 Swiss demonstration reported several benefits from supplying addicts with heroin, including less drug use and crime as well as better health, psychological well-being, and social skills. But these results are based primarily on unverified reports made by the participants themselves. No systematic verification of their claims was made by, say, regular urine screening, HIV testing, or examination of police records. Nevertheless, 18 months into the program, by the unverified accounts of the participants, fully 52 percent of them were using cocaine and a similar number were still using illicit heroin.

The Swiss demonstration, which boasted a retention rate of 69 percent after 18 months, counted as "retained" any participant who periodically returned to the program, no matter how infrequently. Those who dropped out were mostly longtime heroin addicts, heavy cocaine users, or HIV positive. Thus, the demonstration tended to lose those clients with the most severe addiction-related problems—the very persons for whom the experiment was designed. Moreover, although the demonstration was supposed to target hard-core heroin addicts, nearly 20 percent of participants were not heroin users when they entered the program. For a number of reasons, including the unverified self-reports and the lack of appropriate control groups, the demonstration falls far short of scientific standards.

Heroin Maintenance in Britain

For a more balanced look at heroin maintenance, it would seem sensible to consider Britain's prolonged experience rather than Switzerland's brief experiment. In Britain, heroin maintenance has been available for decades, and many physicians are permitted to prescribe it. Yet today, among the nation's estimated 150,000 heroin addicts, 17,000 are receiving oral methadone and fewer than 400 are kept on heroin. The vast majority of British physicians found no compelling evidence that heroin maintenance is useful.

> *"Widespread drug use need not be a fixture of modern life."*

As Mark Kleiman of UCLA has pointed out, "The risk of heroin maintenance is the incentives it provides to 'fail' in other forms of treatment in order to become a publicly supported addict." Addicts characteristically resist treatment and, given the option, choose the least demanding intervention. The most dysfunctional substance abusers are generally deep in denial and rarely enter treatment unless compelled. Thus treatment's first task is overcoming denial and generating the motivation necessary for recovery. Fortunately, today's intensive, supportive, and appropriately demanding methods of rehabilitation are up to this task. Coerced treatment works. Research has demonstrated repeatedly that drug abusers who enter treatment under duress are no less successful than those who enter voluntarily.

Quasi-Legalization of Pot in the Netherlands

Another favorite foreign myth of liberalization advocates comes from the Netherlands, where the quasi-legal status of cannabis products was thought to have narrowed the gateway to adult use of more potent drugs without significantly increasing adolescent use of marijuana. But quasi-legalization of pot in the Netherlands has proven unpopular with the Dutch, who recently demanded a crackdown on the tolerated (though still technically illegal) trade. Although the government still lets coffee shops sell cannabis products, it has slashed the amount permitted for sale or possession from 30 grams to 5 grams and is shutting down shops where heroin or cocaine can be bought.

> *"The vast majority of British physicians found no compelling evidence that heroin maintenance is useful."*

Research has failed to show that quasi-legalization has broken the link between marijuana or hashish use and the use of cocaine. It has, however, revealed an extraordinary increase in marijuana use among Dutch youth between 1984 and 1996 as cannabis policy became increasingly permissive. In 1984, only 4.4 percent of Dutch adolescents had ever used pot. By 1996, 10.6 percent had. In the 18-to-20 age group, lifetime use rose from 15 percent to 44 percent. In this same age group, only 8.5 percent reported using marijuana in the past month in 1984; by 1996, that had jumped to 18.5 percent. Since 1984, cannabis use in the Netherlands has reached rates comparable to those in the United States.

What makes a rising level of marijuana use, particularly by adolescents, so troubling is not just the gateway pot creates to more potent substances. Marijuana itself is far from benign. It can impair short-term memory, deplete energy levels, and impede normal socialization and maturation—all serious matters during adolescence. Moreover, epidemiological studies reveal a significant level of marijuana addiction. Among all users, including casual ones, 9 percent become dependent, as do 20 percent of those whose marijuana use continues beyond experimentation. Most teenagers who receive residential treatment at Phoenix House have used no drug more potent than pot.

True Compassion

Critics of U.S. drug policy argue that simple human compassion requires more lenient drug policies and decriminalizing the possession of drugs. But true compassion demands something quite different. Nadelmann's arguments for reducing the harm to drug users would shield abusers from penalties of their abuse while exacerbating the harm they do their families, their communities, and society itself. A policy that promotes child abuse, domestic violence, the destruction of families, and the devastation of neighborhoods is hardly compassionate.

User-friendly marijuana laws already exist in many states, and there is good reason to press for greater judicial discretion in the sentencing of drug offenders. But no compassionate case can be made for eliminating or significantly diminishing the legal sanctions that now—no matter how imperfectly—limit the spread of drug abuse. Nor can compassion argue for tolerating drug use. When one considers the populations and communities most affected by family dysfunction, social disorder, and violence deriving largely from hard-core substance abuse, the arguments for more lenient drug laws look naive, elitist, or worse.

Dispelling the myths of foreign "successes" would focus the debate on the shortcomings of present U.S. drug policy. With the air cleared of cant, Americans could ask why, with all the talk of a "war on drugs," the United States has never mounted an all-out, all-front assault on illegal drug use.

For a start, such an assault would have to be even-handed. Open-air drug markets could be tolerated no more readily in Harlem, southeast Washington, D.C., or South Central Los Angeles than on Manhattan's Upper East Side or in Georgetown or Brentwood. A serious antidrug policy would call for an equally serious federal investment in drug treatment, which research has consistently found to be cost-effective, with a focus on hard-core users. It would require appropriate treatment for criminals, expand court-mandated treatment, and revise restrictive sentencing laws to make possible more treatment in prison, after prison, and instead of prison. The federal government's prevention campaigns would be sustained, with a more aggressive effort to reach children at risk and increased support

"Since 1984, cannabis use in the Netherlands has reached rates comparable to those in the United States."

for broad community antidrug efforts. Finally, funding for research on abuse and addiction would be raised to a level that reflects drugs' true impact on society and cost to the nation. America has not yet begun to fight a real war on drugs, but that is hardly a reason to surrender.

Chapter 3

Should Marijuana
Laws Be Relaxed?

Chapter Preface

In recent years, several states have passed or narrowly defeated referendums legalizing the use of marijuana for medical purposes. In 1996, Arizona and California became the first states to pass such laws. In 1998, Alaska, Nevada, Oregon, and Washington passed their own medical marijuana initiatives, and voters in Arizona chose to validate their 1996 decision. Polls suggest that voters in Colorado and the District of Columbia approved similar measures in 1998; however, the Colorado initiative was invalidated by the secretary of state, and the D.C. vote was never counted due to Congress's refusal to fund the certification process. These events have further intensified an already heated debate over the legalization of marijuana as medicine.

Proponents of medical marijuana insist that the drug is beneficial in the treatment of many disorders—especially chemotherapy-induced nausea and AIDS wasting syndrome, but also glaucoma, pain, and seizures. While the main therapeutic component of marijuana (THC) is legally available in pill form (Marinol), medical marijuana activists maintain that the full benefits of the drug can only be obtained by smoking it. Even the editor of the *New England Journal of Medicine* has come out in favor of medical marijuana, stating, "To prohibit physicians from alleviating pain and suffering by prescribing marijuana for seriously ill patients is misguided, heavy-handed, and inhumane."

Opponents of medical marijuana argue that the medical conditions cited by legalizers can be effectively treated with Marinol and other medications. Moreover, they view efforts to legalize marijuana for medical purposes as a deceptive first step toward legalizing marijuana—and eventually all currently illegal drugs—for general use. They point out that the state initiatives are being heavily funded by one man—billionaire George Soros, an advocate of drug legalization. William J. Bennett and John P. Walters, coauthors of *Body Count: Moral Poverty—and How to Win America's War Against Crime and Drugs*, write that "Soros and company are pursuing a stealth strategy designed to conceal their real agenda: legalizing all drugs."

A much-anticipated 1999 report on the risks and benefits of marijuana as medicine did little to settle medical marijuana debate. The study, commissioned by the federal government and conducted by the Institute of Medicine (IOM), concluded that marijuana is potentially effective at treating some conditions, but recommended the development of a more effective nonsmoked form of the drug. Proponents and critics of medical marijuana cited different sections of the report to support their respective positions. This selective response to a carefully worded scientific document suggests that the debate over medical marijuana, which is the topic of the following chapter, will not be resolved anytime soon.

Marijuana Laws Should Be Relaxed

by Ira Glasser

About the author: *Ira Glasser is the executive director of the American Civil Liberties Union (ACLU), an organization dedicated to defending Americans' Constitutional rights.*

Before January of 1998, no one except his most devoted friends and followers had ever heard of Ross Rebagliati. But this 20-something Canadian snow boarder became an international figure after his hard-won Olympic gold medal was temporarily snatched away from him when a post-event drug screen revealed traces of marijuana metabolites in his urine. After a suspense-filled 48 hours, the Court of Arbitration of Sports decided to return the medal to its rightful owner.

The conclusion to this episode was a surprise to those who have become accustomed to defeat in the arena of marijuana law reform. Along with the passage of a medical marijuana voters' initiative in California and a more broadly worded drug reform initiative in Arizona in November 1996, it is a signal of real progress in an area that has for so long defied reform.

Thirty Years of Struggle

The marijuana issue is not new to the American Civil Liberties Union (ACLU) or its members. We have officially opposed marijuana prohibition since 1968. Since then, some things have changed, but too much has remained the same. In the past 30 years, 10 million people have been arrested for marijuana offenses in the U.S., the vast majority of them for possession and use. Indeed, in 1996 there were 641,600 marijuana arrests in this country, 85% of them for possession; more than in any previous year!

The hopeful news is that after being bombarded for decades with inflammatory and often false drug war rhetoric, the American public seems more receptive to marijuana law reform today than it has in many years. A strong majority has supported the legal availability of medical marijuana at least since 1995, when a poll commissioned by the ACLU revealed that 79% of the public said

Excerpted from "Spotlight: Why Marijuana Law Reform Should Matter to You," by Ira Glasser, *National ACLU Members' Bulletin*, Spring 1998. Reprinted with permission from the ACLU.

they thought it "would be a good idea to legalize marijuana to relieve pain and for other medical uses if prescribed by a doctor."

It's time for the ACLU to move the issue of marijuana reform front and center. During the worst excesses of the war on drugs, the silence of civil libertarians only emboldened our opponents to push through more and more draconian measures and helped create an atmosphere in which politicians were afraid to talk rationally about the marijuana issue. Recent successes have already brought about the predictable backlash, including the Clinton Administration's threat to punish California physicians who recommended marijuana to their patients. The ACLU can and should play a major role in fending off the government's efforts to undermine marijuana law reform.

Excessive Government Intrusion

Why should the ACLU and its members care about this issue? First and foremost, because it is wrong in principle for the government to criminalize such personal behavior. A government that cannot make it a crime for an individual to drink a martini should for the same reasons not be permitted to make it a crime to smoke marijuana. John Stuart Mill said it perfectly back in 1857 in his famous essay, "On Liberty": "Over himself," he wrote, "over his own body and mind, the individual is sovereign." And Americans certainly behave as if they believe that: marijuana is the third most popular drug in America after alcohol and nicotine (approxi-

> *"In the past 30 years, 10 million people have been arrested for marijuana offenses in the U.S."*

mately 18 million adults used it in 1997, and ten million are regular smokers).

The criminal prohibition of marijuana thus represents an extraordinary degree of government intrusion into the private, personal lives of those adults who choose to use it. Moreover, marijuana users are not the only victims of such a policy because a government that crosses easily over into this zone of personal behavior will cross over into others. The right to personal autonomy—what Mill called individual sovereignty—in matters of religion, political opinion, sexuality, reproductive decisions, and other private, consensual activities is at risk so long as the state thinks it can legitimately punish people for choosing a marijuana joint over a martini.

Civil Liberties Violations

Second, marijuana prohibition is the cause of a host of other very serious civil liberties violations. Millions of employees in both the public and private sectors are now subject to urinalysis drug testing programs, whether or not they are suspected of using drugs. Marijuana is the most common drug turned up by these "body fluid searches" since it is used by many more people than the other illicit drugs, and is detectable for days or weeks after ingestion (long after it has ceased to have any psychoactive effects). A positive marijuana drug test can lead to suspension, termination and coerced drug treatment, even though it does not measure intoxication or impairment. It is as if you were tested and fired from your job for a drink you had at a party last Saturday night.

The government's seizure and civil forfeiture of people's homes, cars and other assets on the grounds they were "used in the commission of" a marijuana offense is another egregious example. The so-called zero tolerance policy has caused outlandishly dispropor-tionate penalties, like the seizure, without trial, of an automobile be-cause a single marijuana joint was found in the glove compartment. People's homes and other posses-sions have been seized and sold, all

> *"A government that cannot make it a crime for an individual to drink a martini should . . . not be permitted to make it a crime to smoke marijuana."*

without a trial. Forfeiture can take place even when no criminal charges are brought, and it is then the individual's burden to petition a court for the return of his or her property. Often the police quickly sell the seized asset and pocket the money for general departmental use.

Ever since 1937, when it adopted the "Marihuana Tax Act," the government has justified the criminalization of marijuana use on the grounds that it is a dan-gerous drug. But this claim looks more and more ludicrous with each passing year. Every independent commission appointed to look into this claim has found that marijuana is relatively benign. For example, President Nixon's Na-tional Commission on Marihuana and Drug Abuse concluded in 1972 that "there is little proven danger of physical or psychological harm from the experi-mental or intermittent use of natural preparations of cannabis," and recom-mended that marijuana for personal use be decriminalized. Ten years later, the National Academy of Sciences issued its finding that "over the past forty years, marijuana has been accused of causing an array of anti-social effects including . . . provoking crime and violence . . . leading to heroin addiction . . . and de-stroying the American work ethic in young people. [These] beliefs . . . have not been substantiated by scientific evidence."

Now here we are in 1998 and the government, along with anti-marijuana or-ganizations like the Partnership for a Drug Free America, still persist in distort-ing the evidence, claiming, for example, that marijuana "kills brain cells" and that it is a "gateway" to hard drugs like cocaine and heroin. These fear tactics are a linchpin in the government's effort to maintain prohibition and the civil liberties violations that flow from it.

Working for Reform

With the continued support of our members, the ACLU will play an active role in bringing about genuine marijuana law reform. Our litigation efforts to end suspicionless drug testing of workers and students, to challenge civil forfeiture laws and to defend the First Amendment right of doctors to recommend marijuana to their patients will all continue, and we hope to establish a special project in the national office to bring legal challenges against other civil liberties violations brought about by prohibition. Our lobbyists at both the state and national levels will continue to oppose repressive legislation and support reform, like Representative Barney Frank's medical marijuana bill [which would make it legal under federal law for doctors to prescribe marijuana]. And we will work hard to educate the public as well, through media relations, publications and other forms of outreach.

ACLU members, too, have a critical role to play. This is a debate that needs to take place in every community. Fundamental questions about individual freedom and limits on government power need to be addressed. You can write letters to your local newspapers and let your elected representatives at all levels know what you think.

Marijuana Should Be Decriminalized

by Lynn Zimmer

About the author: *Lynn Zimmer is an associate professor of sociology at Queens College in New York and coauthor (with John P. Morgan) of* Marijuana Myths, Marijuana Facts: A Review of the Scientific Evidence.

A friend of mine allows his teenage son to smoke marijuana. The boy gets intense nausea from the chemotherapy for his cancer, and marijuana works better than the medications prescribed by his physician. My accountant, a 35-year-old man with AIDS, smokes marijuana before dinner to stimulate his appetite and help him gain weight. A 77-year-old woman who lives near my mother smokes marijuana to treat her glaucoma. A multiple-sclerosis patient, whom I met at a conference, told me he uses marijuana to reduce muscle spasticity.

Under federal law and the laws of most states, these people are committing criminal offenses. In 1996, voters in California and Arizona passed referendums to prevent state law-enforcement officials from arresting people who use marijuana as a medicine. Washington-state voters defeated a drug-policy referendum which, among its provisions, allowed patients access to medical marijuana. In exit polls, however, more than half of those voting "no" said they would have voted "yes" if the initiative had been for medical marijuana alone. In 1998, voters in several other states will get to approve or reject proposals to decriminalize marijuana's use as a medicine. Public-opinion poll data available today suggests they overwhelmingly will approve. [Medical marijuana proposals passed in five states in 1998—ed.] Still, unless federal law is changed, medical marijuana will remain illegal throughout the United States.

A Dismal Failure

Federal officials, including drug czar Barry McCaffrey, oppose leniency on the question of medical marijuana claiming it "sends the wrong message" and undermines government efforts to suppress marijuana's recreational use. By all objective measures, these efforts already are a dismal failure. In 1995, federal agents seized 1 million pounds of marijuana along the U.S. border and spent millions of dollars to find and destroy marijuana grown domestically. Nonetheless, the following year McCaffrey's Office of National Drug Control Policy reported that "high-quality marijuana is widely available in all parts of the United States." On government surveys, about 85 percent of high-school seniors say it is "very easy" or "fairly easy" to obtain marijuana—the same as it has been every year since the early seventies.

During the last 20 years, state and local police have arrested nearly 10 million people for marijuana offenses, about 85 percent for possession. Supporters of this approach claim that criminal sanctions keep some people from using marijuana. However, the data show no relationship between the number of arrests for marijuana possession or the severity of sanctions imposed and the number of people who use marijuana.

Following legal changes since the seventies, researchers have compared the rates of marijuana use in states which have decriminalized marijuana with the rates in states which still had criminal sanctions for simple possession. They found no difference. Marijuana use increased throughout the United States during the seventies, irrespective of the policy in individual states. After 1979, marijuana use started declining. This downward trend, like the upward trend that preceded it, occurred in states both with and without criminal penalties for possessing marijuana.

The War on Marijuana

In the mid-eighties, while marijuana use continued to decline, President Reagan launched a new war on marijuana. Congress recriminalized marijuana possession, setting a penalty of one year in federal prison for possessing a single joint (or less) of marijuana—the same penalty as for possessing small amounts of cocaine or heroin. Two of the states that decriminalized marijuana in the seventies—Oregon and Alaska—reinstated criminal penalties for marijuana possession. In addition, Congress and state legislatures created a variety of new civil sanctions which could be applied to persons arrested for marijuana offenses.

> *"About 85 percent of high-school seniors say it is 'very easy' or 'fairly easy' to obtain marijuana."*

Today marijuana offenders, including those charged with simple possession, can be denied college and/or small business loans, farm subsidies, occupational licenses and government grants, contracts and fellowships. More than half the states have enacted "possess a joint/lose your license" laws, which automatically revoke the driver's license of anyone convicted of any marijuana offense, even if it was not driving-related. People on probation or parole for any criminal offense can be returned to prison on the basis of a urine test showing them to be marijuana users. Following a marijuana arrest, government officials can seize people's property, including cash, cars, boats, land and houses. And, they can keep the property even if there never is a criminal conviction.

After remaining fairly stable throughout the eighties, arrests for marijuana offenses increased dramatically during the nineties. In 1992, state and local police arrested about 269,000 people for marijuana possession. In 1996, marijuana-possession arrests exceeded 545,000—nearly a doubling in a five-year period. Arrests for marijuana distribution and sale also in-

> *"Marijuana offenders ... can be denied college and/or small business loans ... and government grants, contracts, and fellowships."*

creased during these years. But about 85 percent of marijuana arrests, the same as always, were for marijuana possession. In New York City, marijuana arrests doubled between 1990 and 1996, reaching 18,000. Most New York City arrests, such as those across the country, are misdemeanor arrests, for either possessing marijuana or smoking marijuana in public.

No Impact on Use

This war on marijuana has had no apparent impact on marijuana's popularity. From 1992 to 1996, while arrests were doubling, the number of adult marijuana users remained stable. During the same five-year period, adolescent marijuana use increased, after declining for more than a decade. In 1992, 8 percent of 12- to 17-year-olds said they had used marijuana during the last year. By 1996, the rate of past-year marijuana use among adolescents had risen to 13 percent.

Rather than admitting defeat, drug warriors argue that more enforcement and tougher penalties for marijuana offenses are needed. Most marijuana users, they say, never get arrested. And those arrested seldom get sent to prison. Instead, judges give marijuana users suspended sentences, put them on probation or sentence them to community service. A real war on marijuana, drug warriors claim, will produce the deterrence that currently is lacking.

The National Commission on Marihuana and Drug Abuse in 1972 decided that whatever marijuana's harms to users, they paled in comparison to the harm of being arrested. In addition, commission members understood that "marginalizing" even a small minority of marijuana users did not serve the best interests of society. Consider, for example, how many of today's political leaders smoked marijuana in their youth. President Clinton, Vice President Gore and House Speaker Newt Gingrich are among them. If, rather than escaping detection, they had been arrested for marijuana possession, what they now refer to as a "youthful mistake" might have ruined their career opportunities.

Minimal Risk

Even if marijuana were a highly dangerous drug, criminalizing its use would do more harm than good. Fortunately, marijuana is far less dangerous than prohibitionists insist. In *Marijuana Myths, Marijuana Facts: A Review of the Scientific Evidence,* coauthor John P. Morgan and I conclude, based on the evidence, that although marijuana is not completely harmless it has an extremely wide margin of safety.

Marijuana's only clear health risk is respiratory damage from smoking, and this risk is confined to long-term, heavy marijuana smokers. Claims of other biological harms—for example, brain damage, infertility and immune-system impairment—are based on animal and cellular studies using doses of marijuana up to 1,000 times the psychoactive dose in humans. None of these harmful effects have ever been found in studies of people who use marijuana. Unlike most other drugs that humans consume, no dose of marijuana is fatal.

All psychoactive drugs are used in an addictive fashion by some people. Marijuana is no exception. However, compared to other drugs, marijuana has a low addictive potential. Using a synthetic cannabinoid drug which resembles marijuana, researchers recently have reported physical withdrawal in animals. However, to achieve this effect, researchers also administered a blocker drug which immediately strips cannabinoids from receptors. When people stop using marijuana, the drug leaves receptors gradually and they do not experience physical withdrawal.

Even without being addicted, some marijuana users use too much—meaning their use interferes with other life events and activities. Such people, overwhelmingly, had troubled lives before they began using marijuana. There is nothing about marijuana, per se, that causes people

> *"From 1992 to 1996, while arrests were doubling, the number of adult marijuana users remained stable.... Adolescent marijuana use increased."*

to become bad students, poor workers or dysfunctional members of society. Nor is there a pharmacological basis for marijuana's long-alleged "gateway effect." People who have used the least-popular drugs, such as heroin and cocaine, tend also to have used more popular drugs, such as alcohol, tobacco, caffeine and marijuana. However, most marijuana users never use another illegal drug. According to government surveys, for every 100 people who have tried marijuana, only one currently is a regular user of cocaine.

The Decriminalization Buzz

The only clear social risk of marijuana is that people will have accidents during the period of intoxication. Marijuana is not as debilitating as alcohol or many prescription medications. Still, during the few hours after using marijuana, most people show some psychomotor impairment. The data indicate that marijuana is not a major contributor to highway accidents. Nonetheless, criminalizing marijuana-impaired driving makes good social sense. A public-service campaign of the sort now used to deter alcohol-impaired driving might also prove useful. A disadvantage of strict prohibition, which defines all marijuana use as equally wrong and equally illegal, is that it makes such a campaign practically impossible. An advantage of decriminalizing marijuana is that it would allow the dissemination of rules for safer marijuana use.

"Even if marijuana were a highly dangerous drug, criminalizing its use would do more harm than good."

In the current political climate, government officials won't even discuss marijuana decriminalization as an option. But outside government circles, the country is buzzing with decriminalization conversations. Recent public-opinion polls show that half of adults favor eliminating criminal penalties for marijuana possession and use. Nearly three-quarters support immediate removal of the federal ban on marijuana's medical use. They understand, even if government officials don't, that the war on marijuana is unjust, ineffective, unnecessary and far too costly.

Marijuana Should Be Legalized for Medical Purposes

by Lester Grinspoon

About the author: *Lester Grinspoon is an associate professor of psychiatry at Harvard Medical School.*

In September 1928 Alexander Fleming returned from vacation to his laboratory and discovered that one of the petri dishes he had inadvertently left out over the summer was overgrown with staphylococci except for the area surrounding a mold colony. That mold contained a substance he later named penicillin. He published his finding in 1929, but the discovery was ignored by the medical establishment, and bacterial infections continued to be a leading cause of death. Had it aroused the interest of a pharmaceutical firm, its development might not have been delayed. More than 10 years later, under wartime pressure to develop antibiotic substances to supplement sulfonamide, Howard Florey and Ernst Chain initiated the first clinical trial of penicillin (with six patients) and began the systematic investigations that might have been conducted a decade earlier.

Another Wonder Drug?

After its debut in 1941, penicillin rapidly earned a reputation as "the wonder drug of the '40s." There were three major reasons for that reputation: it was remarkably non-toxic, even at high doses; it was inexpensive to produce on a large scale; and it was extremely versatile, acting against the microorganisms that caused a great variety of diseases, from pneumonia to syphilis. In all three respects cannabis suggests parallels:

1) Cannabis is remarkably safe. Although not harmless, it is surely less toxic than most of the conventional medicines it could replace if it were legally available. Despite its use by millions of people over thousands of years, cannabis

Excerpted from testimony given by Lester Grinspoon before the U.S. House of Representatives, Committee on the Judiciary, Subcommittee on Crime, October 1, 1997, Washington, D.C.

has never caused an overdose death. The most serious concern is respiratory system damage from smoking, but that can easily be addressed by increasing the potency of cannabis and by developing the technology to separate the particulate matter in marihuana smoke from its active ingredients, the cannabinoids (prohibition, incidentally, has prevented this technology from flourishing). Once cannabis regains the place in the U.S. Pharmacopoeia that it lost in 1941 after the passage of the Marihuana Tax Act (1937), it will be among the least toxic substances in that compendium. Right now the

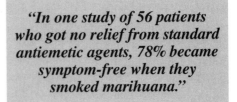

"In one study of 56 patients who got no relief from standard antiemetic agents, 78% became symptom-free when they smoked marihuana."

greatest danger in using marihuana medically is the illegality that imposes a great deal of anxiety and expense on people who are already suffering.

2) Medical cannabis would be extremely inexpensive. Street marihuana today costs $200 to $400 an ounce, but the prohibition tariff accounts for most of that. A reasonable estimate of the cost of cannabis as a medicine is $20 to $30 an ounce, or about 30 to 40 cents per marihuana cigarette. As an example of what this means in practice, consider the following. Both the marihuana cigarette and an 8 mg ondansetron pill—cost to the patient, $30 to $40—are effective in most cases for the nausea and vomiting of cancer chemotherapy (although many patients find less than one marihuana cigarette to be more useful, and they often require several ondansetron pills). Thus cannabis would be at least 100 times less expensive than the best present treatment for this symptom.

3) Cannabis is remarkably versatile. Let me review briefly some of the symptoms and syndromes for which it is useful.

Cancer Treatment

Cannabis has several uses in the treatment of cancer. As an appetite stimulant, it can help to slow weight loss in cancer patients. It may also act as a mood elevator. But the most common use is the prevention of nausea and vomiting of cancer chemotherapy. About half of patients treated with anticancer drugs suffer from severe nausea and vomiting, which are not only unpleasant but a threat to the effectiveness of the therapy. Retching can cause tears of the esophagus and rib fractures, prevent adequate nutrition, and lead to fluid loss. Some patients find the nausea so intolerable they say they would rather die than go on. The antiemetics most commonly used in chemotherapy are metoclopramide (Reglan), the relatively new ondansetron (Zofran), and the newer granisetron (Kytril). Unfortunately, for many cancer patients these conventional antiemetics do not work at all or provide little relief.

The suggestion that cannabis might be useful arose in the early 1970s when some young patients receiving cancer chemotherapy found that marihuana smoking reduced their nausea and vomiting. In one study of 56 patients who got no relief from standard antiemetic agents, 78% became symptom-free when they smoked marihuana. Oral tetrahydrocannabinol (THC) has proved effective where the standard drugs were not. But smoking generates faster and more predictable results because it raises THC concentration in the blood more easily to the needed level. Also, it may be hard for a nauseated patient to take oral medicine. In fact, there is strong evidence that most patients suffering from nausea and vomiting prefer smoked marihuana to oral THC.

Oncologists may be ahead of other physicians in recognizing the therapeutic potential of cannabis. In the spring of 1990, two investigators randomly selected more than 2,000 members of the American Society of Clinical Oncology (one-third of the membership) and mailed them an anonymous questionnaire to learn their views on the use of cannabis in cancer chemotherapy. Almost half of the recipients responded. Although the investigators acknowledge that this group was self-selected and that there might be a response bias, their results provide a rough estimate of the views of specialists on the use of Marinol (dronabinol, oral synthetic THC) and smoked marihuana.

Only 43% said the available legal antiemetic drugs (including Marinol) provided adequate relief to all or most of their patients, and only 46% said the side effects of these drugs were rarely a serious problem. Forty-four percent had recommended the illegal use of marihuana to at least one patient, and half would prescribe it to some patients if it were legal. On average, they considered smoked marihuana more effective than Marinol and roughly as safe.

Glaucoma and Seizures

Cannabis may also be useful in the treatment of glaucoma, the second leading cause of blindness in the United States. In this disease, fluid pressure within the eyeball increases until it damages the optic nerve. About a million Americans suffer from the form of glaucoma (open angle) treatable with cannabis. Marihuana causes a dose-related, clinically significant drop in intraocular pressure that lasts several hours in both normal subjects and those with the abnormally high ocular tension produced by glaucoma. Oral or intravenous THC has the same effect, which seems to be specific to cannabis derivatives rather than simply a result of sedation. Cannabis does not cure the disease, but it can retard the progressive loss of sight when conventional medication fails and surgery is too dangerous.

"There are many case reports of marihuana smokers using the drug to reduce pain: post-surgery pain, headache, migraine, . . . and so on."

About 20% of epileptic patients do not get much relief from conventional anticonvulsant medications. Cannabis has been explored as an alternative at least since 1975 when a case was reported in which marihuana smoking, together with the standard anticonvulsants phenobarbital and diphenylhydantoin, was apparently necessary to control seizures in a young epileptic man. The cannabis derivative that is most promising as an anticonvulsant is cannabidiol. In one controlled study, cannabidiol in addition to prescribed anticonvulsants produced improvement in seven patients with grand mal convulsions; three showed great improvement. Of eight patients who received a placebo instead, only one improved. There are patients suffering from both grand mal and partial seizure disorders who find that smoked marihuana allows them to lower the doses of conventional anticonvulsant medications or dispense with them altogether.

Pain

There are many case reports of marihuana smokers using the drug to reduce pain: post-surgery pain, headache, migraine, menstrual cramps, and so on. Ironically, the best alternative analgesics are the potentially addictive and lethal opioids. In particular, marihuana is becoming increasingly recognized as a drug of choice for the pain that accompanies muscle spasm, which is often chronic and debilitating, especially in paraplegics, quadriplegics, other victims of traumatic nerve injury, and people suffering from multiple sclerosis or cerebral palsy. Many of them have discovered that cannabis not only allows them to avoid the risks of other drugs, but also reduces muscle spasms and tremors; sometimes they are even able to leave their wheelchairs.

"Marihuana is particularly useful for patients who suffer from AIDS because it not only relieves nausea but retards weight loss by enhancing appetite."

One of the most common causes of chronic pain is osteoarthritis, which is usually treated with synthetic analgesics. The most widely used of these drugs—aspirin, acetaminophen (Tylenol), and nonsteroidal antiinflammatory drugs (NSAIDs) like ibuprofen and naproxen— are not addictive, but they are often insufficiently powerful. Furthermore, they have serious side effects. Stomach bleeding and ulcer induced by aspirin and NSAIDs are the most common serious adverse drug reactions reported in the United States, causing an estimated 7,000 deaths each year. Acetaminophen can cause liver damage or kidney failure when used regularly for long periods of time; a recent study suggests it may account for 10% of all cases of end-stage renal disease, a condition that requires dialysis or a kidney transplant. Marihuana, as I pointed out earlier, has never been shown to cause death or serious illness.

AIDS

More than 300,000 Americans have died of AIDS. Nearly a million are infected with HIV, and at least a quarter of a million have AIDS. Although the spread of AIDS has slowed among homosexual men, the reservoir is so huge that the number of cases is sure to grow. Women and children as well as both heterosexual and homosexual men are now being affected; the disease is spreading most rapidly among intravenous drug abusers and their sexual partners. The disease can be attacked with anti-viral drugs, of which the best known are zidovudine (AZT) and protease inhibitors. Unfortunately, these drugs sometimes cause severe nausea that heightens the danger of semi-starvation for patients who are already suffering from nausea and losing weight because of the illness—a condition sometimes called the AIDS wasting syndrome.

> *"In the 1970s the public began to rediscover [marihuana's] medical value."*

Marihuana is particularly useful for patients who suffer from AIDS because it not only relieves the nausea but retards weight loss by enhancing appetite. When it helps patients regain lost weight, it can prolong life. Marinol has been shown to relieve nausea and retard or reverse weight loss in patients with HIV infection, but most patients prefer smoked cannabis for the same reasons that cancer chemotherapy patients prefer it: it is more effective and has fewer unpleasant side effects, and the dosage is easier to adjust.

A Medicine with a Long History

These are the symptoms and syndromes for which cannabis is most commonly used today, but there are others for which clinical experience provides compelling evidence. It is distressing to consider how many lives might have been saved if penicillin had been developed as a medicine immediately after Fleming's discovery. It is equally frustrating to consider how much suffering might have been avoided if cannabis had been available as a medicine for the last 60 years. Initial enthusiasm for drugs is often disappointed after further investigation, but this is hardly likely in the case of cannabis, since it is not a new medicine at all. Its long medical history began 5,000 years ago in China and extended well into the twentieth century. Between 1840 and 1900, more than one hundred papers on its therapeutic uses were published in American and European medical journals. It was recommended as an appetite stimulant, muscle relaxant, analgesic, sedative, anticonvulsant, and treatment for opium addiction. As late as 1913, the great Sir William Osler cited it as the best remedy for migraine in a standard medical textbook.

In the United States, what remained of marihuana's medical use was effectively eliminated by the Marihuana Tax Act of 1937, which was ostensibly designed to prevent nonmedical use but made cannabis so difficult to obtain that it was removed from standard pharmaceutical references. When the present comprehensive federal drug law was passed in 1970, marihuana was officially classified as a Schedule I drug: a high potential for abuse, no accepted medical use, and lack of safety for use under medical supervision.

But in the 1970s the public began to rediscover its medical value, as letters appeared in lay publications from people who had learned that it could relieve their asthma, nausea, muscle spasms, or pain and wanted to share that knowledge with readers who were familiar with the drug. The most effective spur to the movement for medical marihuana came from the discovery that it could prevent the AIDS wasting syndrome. It is not surprising that the Physicians Association for AIDS Care was one of the medical organizations that endorsed the 1996 California initiative prohibiting criminal prosecution of medical marihuana users. The mid-1980s had already seen the establishment, often by people with AIDS, of cannabis buyers' clubs, organizations that distribute medical marihuana in open defiance of the law. These clubs buy marihuana wholesale and provide it to patients at or near cost, usually on the written recommendation of a physician. Although a few of the clubs have been raided and closed, most are still flourishing, and new ones are being organized. Some of them may gain legal status as a result of the initiative.

Reform Efforts

Until the 1996 vote in California, efforts to change the laws had been futile. In 1972 the National Organization for the Reform of Marihuana Laws (NORML) entered a petition to move marihuana out of Schedule I under federal law so that it could become a prescription drug. It was not until 1986 that the Drug Enforcement Administration (DEA) finally agreed to the public hearings required by law. During two years of hearings, many patients and physicians testified and thousands of pages of documentation were introduced. In 1988 the DEA's Administrative Law Judge, Francis L. Young, declared that marihuana fulfilled the requirement for transfer to Schedule II. In his opinion he described it as "one of the safest therapeutically active substances known to man." His order was overruled by the DEA.

"The FDA . . . ignored the data that suggested that smoked marihuana was more useful than oral THC for some patients."

Nevertheless, a few patients have been able to obtain medical marihuana legally in the last twenty years. Beginning in the 1970s, thirty-five states passed legislation that would have permitted medical use of cannabis but for the federal law. Several of those states actually established special research programs, with the permission of the federal government, under which patients who were receiving cancer chemotherapy would be allowed to use cannabis. These projects demonstrated the value of both smoked marihuana and oral THC. The FDA then approved oral THC as a prescription medicine, but ignored the data that suggested that smoked marihuana was more useful than oral THC for some patients. With the approval of Marinol, this research came to an end. In 1976, the federal government introduced the Individual Treatment Investigational New Drug program (commonly referred to as the Compassionate IND), which provided marihuana to a few patients whose doctors were willing to undergo the paperwork-burdened and time-consuming application process. About three dozen patients eventually received marihuana before the program was discontinued in 1992, and eight survivors are still receiving it—the only persons in the country for whom it is not a forbidden medicine. It is safe to say that a significant number of the more than ten million American citizens arrested on marihuana charges in the last thirty years were using the drug therapeutically. The Schedule I classification persists, although in my view and the view of millions of other Americans, it is medically absurd, legally questionable, and morally wrong.

The Validity of the Evidence

Opponents of medical marihuana often object that the evidence of its usefulness, although strong, comes only from case reports and clinical experience. It is true that there are no double-blind controlled studies meeting the standards of the Food and Drug Administration, chiefly because legal, bureaucratic, and financial obstacles have been constantly put in the way. The situation is ironical, since so much research has been done on marihuana, often in unsuccessful efforts to show health hazards and addictive potential, that we know more about it than about most prescription drugs. In any case, individual therapeutic responses are often obscured in group experiments, and case reports and clinical experience are the source of much of our knowledge of drugs. As Dr. Louis Lasagna has pointed out, controlled experiments were not needed to recognize the therapeutic potential of chloral hydrate, barbiturates, aspirin, insulin, or penicillin. Nor was that the way we learned about the use of propranolol for hypertension, diazepam for status epilepticus, and imipramine for enuresis. All these drugs had originally been approved for other purposes.

In the experimental method known as the single patient randomized trial, active and placebo treatments are administered randomly in alternation or succession. The method is often used when large-scale controlled studies are inappropriate because the disorder is rare, the patient is atypical, or the response to treatment is idiosyncratic. Several patients have told me that they assured themselves of marihuana's effectiveness by carrying out such experiments on themselves, alternating periods of cannabis use with periods of abstention. I am convinced that the medical reputation of cannabis is derived partly from similar experiments conducted by many other patients.

"Years of effort devoted to showing that marihuana is exceedingly dangerous have proved the opposite."

Some physicians may regard it as irresponsible to advocate use of a medicine on the basis of case reports, which are sometimes disparaged as merely "anecdotal" evidence which counts apparent successes and ignore apparent failures. That would be a serious problem only if cannabis were a dangerous drug. The years of effort devoted to showing that marihuana is exceedingly dangerous have proved the opposite. It is safer, with fewer serious side effects, than most prescription

148

medicines, and far less addictive or subject to abuse than many drugs now used as muscle relaxants, hypnotics, and analgesics.

The Benefits Outweigh the Risks

Thus cannabis should be made available even if only a few patients could get relief from it, because the risks would be so small. For example, as I mentioned, many patients with multiple sclerosis find that cannabis reduces their muscle spasms and pain. A physician may not be sure that such a patient will get more relief from marihuana than from the standard drugs baclofen, dantrolene, and diazepam—all of which are potentially dangerous or addictive—but it is almost certain that a serious toxic reaction to marihuana will not occur. Therefore the potential benefit is much greater than any potential risk.

During the past few years, the medical uses of marihuana have become increasingly clear to many physicians and patients, and the number of people with direct experience of these uses has been growing. Therefore the discussion is now turning from whether cannabis is an effective medicine to how it should be made available. It is essential to relax legal restrictions that prevent physicians and patients from achieving a workable accommodation that takes into account the needs of suffering people.

State Medical Marijuana Laws Should Be Respected

by Robert Scheer

About the author: *Robert Scheer is a contributing editor for the* Los Angeles Times *newspaper.*

If there is one stunning bit of stupidity that instantly garners bipartisan support, it's the failed war on drugs. Virtually all politicians march in lock-step to do battle with unmitigated fervor against each and every banned drug as if they were all created equal in destructive potency and anti-social impulse.

Nowhere is the simplistic arrogance that underwrites national drug policy more blatant than in the continual denigration of voters in the states that dare dissent from official policy. In 1996, it was the electorate of California and Arizona that begged to differ and, by voting in favor of the limited legalized use of medical marijuana, incurred the blistering wrath of the anti-drug crusaders.

To hear the uproar in official circles, you would have thought marijuana, even in small quantities and prescribed by doctors for AIDS and chemotherapy patients, was demon rum itself, and that the ghosts of the temperance society ladies had risen from their graves to smash open the doors of the cannabis clubs.

A Sane Electorate

But the hysteria failed. Despite police harassment, the nonstop fulminations of President Bill Clinton's drug czar Barry McCaffrey and a massive advertising campaign against medical marijuana, the electorate has remained sane.

In the 1998 election, voters in Nevada, Oregon, Alaska and Washington joined California and Arizona in approving patient use of marijuana. In Arizona and Oregon, voters moved beyond medical marijuana use, opting for serious steps in the direction of decriminalizing possession of small amounts of marijuana.

Exit polls show that voters in the nation's capital similarly voted for legal use of medical marijuana, but in one of the more egregious violations of the spirit of representative government, Congress approved a ban to even count the D.C. vote on this measure. The fight to prevent the vote count was led by ultra-right wing Rep. Bob Barr (R-Ga.), who perfectly embodies the contradictions inherent in his ideological obsessions. Barr has been the most vociferous opponent of gun control legislation and even gutted an anti-terrorist bill to tag explosives material on the grounds that it would be an unwarranted extension of government power. But locking folks up for smoking weed is his favorite cause.

He's not alone. Marijuana remains the scourge of the $11-billion-a-year anti-drug bureaucracy not because of any documentable antisocial impact but simply because that's where it gets the big numbers of drug users to justify the bloated budgets.

An Absurd Policy

According to FBI statistics, 545,396 Americans were arrested in 1996 for possessing marijuana, a substance that, if legal, would prove no more dangerous to society than the vodka martini one occasionally sips. That doesn't mean it's good to abuse any mood-altering drug, but rather that a national policy which turns the relatively benign use of marijuana into a highly profitable and socially disruptive criminal activity is absurd.

But don't try to tell the politicians that, or they'll tear your head off. Just look at the smear job McCaffrey has done on financier/philanthropist George Soros and other businessmen for daring to help finance recent state ballot initiatives that present voters with a drug policy choice.

McCaffrey thundered recently that the folks putting up money for these campaigns are "a carefully camouflaged, exorbitantly funded, well-heeled elitist group whose ultimate goal is to legalize drug use in the United States." Interesting that McCaffrey was silent on the far larger amounts of tobacco industry money that poured into California to challenge a ballot initiative to increase the tax on tobacco products and divert it to education. It is invidious to pretend that the drugs now classified as legal are less harmful than those whose use is branded as a crime.

Drug abuse, both of legal and illegal drugs, is a medical problem requiring treatment by health professionals, not cops. What makes the war on drugs so nutty is that it's more about maintaining the coercive power of anti-drug bureaucrats than treating those who suffer from serious drug abuse.

"Despite . . . a massive advertising campaign against medical marijuana, the electorate has remained sane."

The voters have been vilified as naive, but that appellation belongs to a war-on-drugs crusade that has filled our jails while leaving illegal drugs more plentiful and cheaper. It drives the anti-drug bureaucracy mad that voters in six states have now voted to ever so slightly challenge its total grip on the awesome power of government, but it bodes well for our representative system of government.

Marijuana Laws Should Not Be Relaxed

by Mark Souder

About the author: *Mark Souder, a Republican congressman from Indiana, is vice chairman of the House Government Reform and Oversight Subcommittee on National Security.*

Rolling Stone magazine noted in its May 5, 1994, issue that currency speculator and billionaire philanthropist George Soros gave the Drug Policy Foundation, one of many recipients of his "charitable" largesse, suggestions to follow if they wanted his assistance: "[H]ire someone with the political savvy to sit down and negotiate with government officials and target a few winnable issues, like medical marijuana and the repeal of mandatory minimums." Keith Stroup, founder of the National Organization for the Reform of Marijuana Laws, or NORML, told an Emory University audience in 1979 that medicinal marijuana would be used as a red herring to give marijuana a good name. Richard Cowan, writing for the pro-drug *High Times* magazine, described the "medical model as spearheading a strategy for the legalization of marijuana by 1997."

According to public-opinion polls, legalization of marijuana is not supported by the American people. This explains why the drug lobby carefully steers away from using the term "legalization," preferring cryptic terms such as harm reduction, decriminalization and medicalization. The goal of the drug lobby has not changed; it only is camouflaged. The public sensibly and resolutely remains opposed to recreational marijuana use, but drug legalizers shamefully are trying to con voters through deceptive ballot referenda exploiting the ill and dying.

The False Claims of Legalizers

Marijuana legalizers commonly claim America's prisons teem with young people whose only crime was simple possession of marijuana, and that drug arrests disproportionately affect minorities. The recent debate about crack-cocaine sentencing disparities sparked similar claims of racism by the criminal justice system. The drug lobby ignores the obvious fact that a war on drugs hits

inner-city traffickers foremost and helps law-abiding residents of neighborhoods who have the least resources with which to fight back. Despite the in-
escapable conclusion that placing drug dealers behind bars protects neighborhoods against criminals, violent crime and social ills attendant with drug use,
drug legalizers such as University of California at Los Angeles' Mark Kleiman
absurdly claim: "Locking up a bur-
glar does not materially change the
opportunities for other burglars,
while locking up a drug dealer leaves
potential customers for new dealers."
The drug lobby frequently com-
pares the drug war to Prohibition.

> *"According to public-opinion polls, legalization of marijuana is not supported by the American people."*

But as a publication at the turn of the century (when the United States had a
raging drug problem) observed, "a drunkard may retain his moral equilibrium
between debauches . . . but the 'dope fiend,' once thoroughly addicted, inevitably drops into utter debasement." Unlike illegal drugs, alcohol and drinking were embedded in Anglo-Saxon and European social customs. While the
temperance movement prevailed after heated debate, drug restrictions passed
during the same period widely were regarded as uncontroversial and needed.
Western states passed marijuana-prohibition laws in response to a rash of
crimes and violence linked to cannabis use among Mexican immigrants. A
medical exemption existed then to the import of marijuana, but soon states and
politicians appealed to the federal government for help in confronting the "loco
weed." Legendary New York journalist Meyer Berger in 1938 summed up expert medical opinion at the time: "Marijuana, while no more habit-forming than
ordinary cigarette smoking, offers a shorter cut to complete madness than any
other drug."

The Medical Marijuana Movement

Drug legalizers lost a ballot initiative in Washington state on November 4,
1997, a setback from victories to legalize illegal drugs in California and Arizona. The Washington-state referendum—I-685, which failed by a margin of 60
percent to 40 percent—combined the worst aspects of the legalization initiatives in California and Arizona by not only seeking to legalize marijuana but
also cocaine, heroin, LSD and other narcotics on Schedule I of the federal Controlled Substances Act, drugs judged to have no medicinal benefit and high potential for abuse. I-685 also would have released drug offenders from prison.
I-685 was bolstered by millions of dollars in contributions from a handful of
out-of-state millionaires, including Soros—dubbed the "Daddy Warbucks" of
drug legalization by former health, education and welfare secretary Joe Califano—and Arizona millionaire John Sperling. The measure failed even though
drug legalizers outspent antidrug advocates by a ratio of nearly 15-to-1.

Washington state antidrug activists warned against complacency in fighting the legalizers. They acknowledged the battle against I-685 was significantly buoyed by the zealotry of the legalizers to delist Schedule I substances and by the National Rifle Association's successful multimillion-dollar campaign against a gun-control referendum also on the ballot.

The District of Columbia is threatened with a marijuana "medicalization" initiative in November 1998, sponsored by a homosexual advocacy organization, the AIDS Coalition to Unleash Power. AIDS activists should take note of pioneering research by Dr. Thomas Klein at the University of South Florida who showed marijuana alters the immune system and may accelerate HIV-infection into full-blown AIDS cases. D.C.'s Measure 57 would permit up to 20 people to cultivate and sell unlimited quantities of marijuana for an individual suffering from an amorphous range of conditions—essentially shielding drug dealers from prosecution. [The D.C. measure failed after Congress refused to provide funds to certify the results.—ed.]

As drug czar Barry McCaffrey argues, the ballot box is the wrong place for decisions about efficacy and safety of medicines. The Food and Drug Administration, or FDA, was created to protect the public against snake-oil salesmen, and consumer-safety laws require proper labeling of ingredients and dosages. The sale of crude marijuana circumvents those protections.

Bad Medicine

The pro-drug lobby successfully described Proposition 215 in California as "medical" marijuana for the sick and dying, preying on the compassionate nature of the American people, but Prop. 215 legalized marijuana with no age limitation for "any illness for which marijuana provides relief," including ailments of dubious nature and severity such as memory recall, writers cramp and corn callouses. The FDA has approved the only psychoactive ingredient of marijuana, THC, found useful for pain relief as Marinol, in pill form through prescription. Marinol, a Schedule II drug with limited medical use and high potential for abuse, is an antinausea drug for cancer patients who fail to respond to other drugs, and an appetite stimulant for people suffering from AIDS wasting syndrome. THC has not, however, been shown to be safe and effective for any other condition other than nausea and wasting due to AIDS. In a double-blind study, patients preferred Marinol over smoking marijuana 2-to-1. A marijuana study by the Institute of Medicine concluded risks of marijuana on the immune system were

"Marijuana alters the immune system and may accelerate HIV-infection into full-blown AIDS."

such that it favored development of a smoke-free inhaled delivery system to provide purer forms of THC, or its related compound, cannabinoids.

The drug lobby, however, rejects legal use of THC in Marinol and continues to promote use of crude marijuana cigarettes as medicine. One doctor, explaining why marijuana is not medicine, gave the analog of eating moldy bread in an attempt to get penicillin. A prominent oncologist professed he could manage pain with legal drugs in 99 percent of his patients, and that there are newer and better medications for chemotherapy patients than Marinol, describing one, Zofran, as a "miracle" drug.

Crude marijuana consists of more than 400 chemicals which, when smoked, become thousands of chemicals. Drugs from a pharmacy are of a single ingredient and of a known dosage. Pot advocates often cite the fact that morphine, available under a doctor's care, is a heroin derivative. What they neglect to mention is that morphine received FDA approval and underwent rigorous clinical testing, a public-safety standard approved drugs must meet.

> *"A prominent oncologist professed he could manage pain with legal drugs in 99 percent of his patients."*

Drug legalizers often cite Americans participating in an ongoing federal experiment at the University of Mississippi to evaluate any benefit from medicinal marijuana, implying that the federal government believes marijuana could be medicinal. But to date, despite 12,000 studies of the medical utility of marijuana, an overwhelming consensus exists in the scientific community that smoked marijuana never can be a medicine. The federal experimental program, consisting of eight people, has declined new admissions since 1992. Congress, in its reauthorization of the drug-czar's office, banned further studies of marijuana as medicine, a provision which I sponsored.

A Harmful Drug

While the Clinton administration campaigns vigorously against cigarettes and chides the tobacco industry for its marketing techniques, marijuana cigarettes rarely are targets of condemnation. Ironically, the tobacco industry, like the drug lobby today, once promoted cigarettes as medicine until the Federal Trade Commission halted this practice in 1955.

Marijuana is addictive, leading to the use of other drugs such as cocaine and heroin, and is a major cause of accidents and injuries. It can cause respiratory disease and mental disorders including depression, paranoia, decreased cognitive performance and impaired memory. Babies born to women who smoked marijuana during pregnancy have an increased incidence of leukemia, low birth weight and other newborn abnormalities. The National Institute of Drug Abuse's director frequently mentions brain scans showing that lower cerebral activity seems to account for some of the reported learning disturbances found in chronic marijuana users.

As a *New York Times* editorial recently put it, parents need to realize today's marijuana is more potent than the version they may have smoked in their youth, and "research has shown the drug to be far more dangerous to young people than was known in the 1960s and 1970s, with a higher THC content. It can be particularly harmful to the growth and development of teenagers."

There is a solid reason for scientific studies and FDA approval—to avoid medical catastrophes such as thalidomide. Good medicine is not conceived at the polls, but through routine clinical trials. Since marijuana is far more carcinogenic than tobacco cigarettes, it's not compassionate to recommend it to sick people—it's cruel.

Marijuana Should Not Be Legalized for Medical Purposes

by Charles Krauthammer

About the author: *Charles Krauthammer is a syndicated columnist.*

Take any morally dubious proposition—like assisting a suicide—and pretend it is merely help for the terminally ill, and you are well on your way to legitimacy and a large public following. That is how assisted suicide is sold. That is how the legalization of marijuana is sold. Indeed, that is precisely how Proposition 215, legalizing marijuana for medical use, passed in November 1996 in California.

The Prop 215 ad campaign dwelt on the medicinal uses of marijuana for AIDS and cancer, neatly skirting the clause in the referendum that legalizes it for "any other illness." And now the *New England Journal of Medicine* has taken up the refrain, with its editor-in-chief, Dr. Jerome Kassirer, editorializing passionately in favor of giving marijuana to those "at death's door" who want it.

Treatment for Potheads

The problem with Dr. Kassirer's argument is that people who are toking up at the many "cannabis buyers' clubs" that immediately opened as a result of Prop 215 are not at all at death's door. As Hanna Rosin reports in the *New Republic,* the clubs are peopled not by the desperate terminally ill but by a classic cross section of California potheads, all conveniently citing some diagnosis or other—migraines, insomnia, stress—as their ticket to Letheland.

Marijuana gives them a buzz, all right. But medical effects? Be serious. The medical effects of marijuana for these conditions are nil. They are, as everyone involved in the enterprise knows—and as many behind Prop 215 intended—a fig leaf for legalization.

Even for the truly seriously ill, the medical claims for marijuana are dubious. Which is, I suspect, why Dr. Kassirer is so dismissive and defensive about having real clinical trials that test whether marijuana does anything more than a placebo.

Glaucoma? It borders on malpractice to give marijuana for glaucoma. While it can reduce intraocular pressure (with huge doses of pot), it also can constrict blood supply to the optic nerve, exacerbating vision problems. There are far safer and better drugs. Cancer and AIDS? Marijuana may

> *"Even for the truly seriously ill, the medical claims for marijuana are dubious."*

reduce nausea and anorexia—the familiar "munchies" that many will remember from the 1960s—but there are effective drugs on the market that do an equal or better job.

What marijuana uniquely offers the seriously ill is not "medical" effects—which are either nonexistent or easily duplicated by other drugs—but a high and good feeling.

That doesn't alarm me. Who can begrudge the terminally ill temporary escape from their terror and misery? I don't. But I do object to the pretense about medical effects. Marijuana is not particularly good medicine. It is recreation and relief.

The Slippery Slope

Not surprisingly the disingenuousness is contagious. The president's drug czar pretends that the reason he opposes marijuana for terminal patients is, to quote his public affairs person on "Nightline," "to make sure that you provide the best medicine."

But that is surely not the real reason. The administration would hardly launch a huge public relations and enforcement campaign against patients who were popping, say, an inferior anti-nausea pill. The real reason is the slippery slope. The administration is involved because once you start with marijuana for the ill, you end up with marijuana for anybody who can claim to be ill, which, as the cannabis clubs demonstrate, opens the door to anyone.

And that societal nod and wink sends a message to kids that pot is okay. Children are extraordinarily sensitive to signals coming from the culture. In the '80s, when marijuana wasn't cool, when it was denounced and derided, its use went into decline. In the '90s, with no message coming from the political authorities—read: grownups—and a revival of marijuana cool in music and mass media, its use among teens has risen dramatically.

Anyone who has worked with drug abusers knows the havoc that marijuana—particularly marijuana as a gateway drug to harder stuff such as cocaine and heroin—can wreak in the lives of kids. Why, even George Soros, sugar daddy of the legalization movement, admits that "marijuana can be harmful to the mental and emotional development of youngsters."

What to do? Start with honesty. For the truly terminally ill, let them take marijuana—or LSD or heroin or whatever else they want. But only the terminally ill. And only in supervised medical settings, say, a room in a hospital. (The No Smoking signs would have to be taken down.)

As for the rest—no go. The cannabis clubs are a sham, an invitation to every teenager with a hangnail to come in and zone out. Close them.

You object? Want to legalize pot for everyone? Fine. Make your case. But no more hiding behind the terminally ill.

The Medical Marijuana Movement Seeks to Legitimize All Marijuana Use

by Hanna Rosin

About the author: *Hanna Rosin is a staff writer for the* Washington Post *newspaper.*

Opening day at San Francisco's Cannabis Cultivators Club, and the line at the door eats up the whole block. It is a well-mannered line, considering who is standing in it: a bunch of homeless men streaked with grime, a very large and fierce-looking woman in a wheelchair, a gaggle of mulatto transvestites. Near the front of the line, a woman with pronounced buck teeth is straining, with slow and deliberate jabs, to place a feather earring in the ear of the man standing in front of her, a difficult task given that the man has no ear, merely a gnarled nub of cartilage. She giggles; Van Gogh smiles. A tall, gaunt man guards the door. He checks to see that each person has a letter of diagnosis from a doctor, legally qualifying him or her to buy marijuana. The gatekeeper is calm, composed, and so are the men and women that file silently past him. . . .

Relaunching the Mothership

Inside the club, order seems to reign, as well. The computers are up, the phones are ringing. Reporters chase down sick people in wheelchairs. The reporters are here because today is a news event: the relaunching of the mothership, as the club is known to its grateful patients, marks the coming out of California's medical marijuana movement after years in hiding. Founded in 1992, the club existed in an uneasy truce with the city of San Francisco, selling pot to some 12,000 customers designated as medical patients. It grew to become by far the largest medical marijuana club in the state, serving as many patients in a day as the other seven or so clubs together might serve in a week. Then, in August, 1996, state narcotics agents raided the club and shut it down on a host of marijuana possession and distribution charges. Three months later, California voters, by a margin of 56 to 44 percent, passed Proposition 215: The Medical Marijuana Initiative, making it legal to smoke marijuana in California with the approval or recommendation of a doctor. A local judge promptly gave the club permission to reopen and designated the club's owner, a former (and often-convicted)

> *"The [medical marijuana] movement is about the compassionate extension of relief to sick people . . . but it is also very much, and primarily, about legalization."*

marijuana dealer named Dennis Peron, as a caregiver (which is to say, pot provider) for up to 12,000 patients.

Today is the first day of the new era, and Peron is eager to make a good, caregiving sort of impression. Dressed in an argyle sweater and blue oxford with a pinstriped tie, he glides to the middle of the room, climbs up on a coffee table ringed with doting patients and speaks: "If we can't get in touch with your doctor we can't sell you marijuana. We are law makers, not law breakers." He then adds, with a mixture of melodrama and mock asides, "We will never abandon you. We will save the people in pain. Once you get your card, you will see the marijuana smoke. Just like the old days. Oh, that smell. . . ."

A cynical listener might discern here an attitude that seems less like that of the nurturing caregiver, and more like that of, how to put it, an old pothead eager for the good times to roll again. The cynical listener would be on to something. Late in the afternoon, when all the reporters have cleared out to meet their daily deadline, Peron hushes the crowd again. "I know a lot of you have waited a long time and you are sick and you have to go through this bullshit. And it is bullshit. Today we have to go through this bullshit for a thousand years of love. I've missed you so much. One week of bullshit, a thousand years of love." One of Peron's deputies rushes outside to carry the message to those who did not make it in that day. "Don't worry," he eases them. "It will be just like before. Just come back tomorrow. Today is the first day so things are a little, you know. Just come back tomorrow."

The Medical Marijuana Campaign

The passage of Proposition 215 surprised even its most zealous supporters. In the months before the November 1996 election, they fought what they thought was an uphill battle against an enemy that tried to portray them as a front for the seedy drug dealers on Market Street. Tough-talking law enforcement officers like Orange County Sheriff Brad Gates warned that the initiative "would legalize marijuana, period!" But the pro-215 activists knew better than to engage in that argument. They stuck to their line: the referendum was simply about limited, medical use of the drug, and then only in extreme cases. They made the debate one of compassion versus suffering, plastering billboards across the state with images of the hollow-faced sick and dying, the bloated and bald Helen Reading, 43, breast cancer; the furrowed and frowning Thomas Carter, 47, epilepsy. "You have just been told you have terminal cancer," reads one poster. "Now for the bad news: your medicine is illegal."

Of equal importance in their electoral victory, the pro-215 activists tailored their image midstream; they hired a pinstriped professional, Bill Zimmerman, to run the campaign, and to run it at a conspicuous distance from people like Dennis Peron: "He was pictured on election night smoking a joint and saying, 'Let's all get stoned and watch election night returns,'" Zimmerman recalls. "That kind of behavior supports the opponents' view that we are a stalking horse for legalization. . . . He could ruin it for the truly sick." Zimmerman's images stuck. The *New York Times* ran a sympathetic portrait of "an arthritic, HIV-positive cabaret performer," under the headline "marijuana club helps those in pain." Sympathetic, and gullible. With its breathy, tenderhearted reporting, the intrepid *Times* reporters implicitly tried to correct Sheriff Gates. See, the article said, these people smoking these joints are cripples, real ones, and cancer patients, real ones. They are merely looking for a little easing of their pain, not fronting for the de facto legalization of pot.

Legitimation Through Medicalization

The truth about the medical marijuana movement is much simpler, and blindingly obvious after a day in Peron's club. The movement is about the compassionate extension of relief to sick people—THC, the active ingredient in marijuana, offers some sick people a cheap, effective surcease from pain—but it is also very much, and primarily, about legalization. The movement may feature billboards of the infirm, but in the offices of its activists you are more likely to find a different poster, a stoner classic: The Declaration of Independence and the U.S. Constitution were written on hemp paper.

Both the hemp poster and the sad faces of Helen Reading and Thomas Carter are, in different ways, part of an overall campaign to make pot wholesome—to turn it into something as legitimate as, say, over-the-counter cough syrup. The medical marijuana movement and the legalization movement share a common language and common idea. Most of the medical marijuana clubs that have sprung up in California are much stricter than Peron's, which represents the outside edge of respectability and adherence to the law.

> *"Legitimation through medicalization is not a novel tactic in drug history."*

These more proper establishments run would-be clientele through the checklist of rigid protocols a patient must submit to—a signed doctor's recommendation, a detailed health questionnaire, follow-up visits to the doctor. But, if you talk to the people who run the clubs for any time at all, you will notice that mostly what they talk about is not medicine but legalization—the same standard jargon of hemp and drug wars and government oppression and narcs. One of the strictest clubs in the state is in Oakland, a small place run by a righteous young man named Jeff Jones, who is rigorous in following the letter of the law. The law says, basically, that marijuana may only be sold to people who have a legitimate medical need for it—people, in other words, who could be made to feel better by a toke or two. "But wouldn't marijuana make anyone feel better?" I asked Jones. "Now you're getting the point," he answered, approvingly.

> *"People who get high are very difficult to interview. . . . They can't complete a thought."*

Legitimation through medicalization is not a novel tactic in drug history. In their times and places, opium, laudanum, cocaine, nicotine, alcohol and LSD have been packaged as cures. At the turn of the century, middle-class medicine cabinets were stocked with doses of morphine, codeine and laudanum. The tincture of opium in spirits was known as "God's own medicine." Fussy baby? Try Children's Comfort, or Mrs. Godfrey's soothing syrup, a healthy shot of opium in wine. Public health officials estimated at the time that one in every 200 Americans was a drug addict, most of them happy (giddy, even) housewives. And now, we have pot, the medicine. . . .

Andrew, Pebbles, and Buzzy

The excitement of a new dawn is felt on this opening day of the club, and it is hardly dampened by the dim, fusty interior. The place is divided into three spacious, though windowless, rooms and looks like the messy common room of a college dorm, with bits of origami and amateur "art" hanging from the ceiling, mismatched couches placed askew, ranging in color from bruised to rust to dung. The first person I run into is Andrew, a middle-aged black man with clipped dreads. "You're a journalist," he observes, when he sees me taking notes. "I keep a journal." Having established this common bond, he feels comfortable showing me some of his work. "Before I started writing, life wasn't worth two puffs of coke," he explains as a prologue. I expect to see some more revelations in the journal, maybe some bad poetry. But all I can make out on the first page is "shorts suck" with a crude drawing of Andrew in boxer shorts.

I try to change the subject, and ask him why he's here. He suffers from a disease not mentioned in the posters, but which turns out to be a relatively common ailment among the club's patients. "I have insomnia," he explains. "Also, I get migraine headaches." Before I can ask Andrew's last name, my arm is grabbed from behind by a woman I soon find out is Pebbles Trippet, a Berkeley activist who wants me to listen to an on-camera interview she's doing with the TV equivalent of *High Times*.

Pebbles is a woman who once was conventionally lovely, with clear blue eyes, a straight nose and long blond hair. She has preserved these features of young beauty—the eyes, the long hair—but added a layer of must and cobwebs and wrinkles. She is draped in what looks like an old rug with pockets, a tattered rainbow lei, cracked leather sandals and mismatched socks. The effect is jarring, like a skeleton with pretty hair. "I am a medical marijuana user," she declares to the camera. "I have self-medicated for decades. They have tried to jail me in three cities—Contra Costa County, Sonoma County, Marin County."

I ask her what's wrong, trying to sound sympathetic.

"I get migraine headaches."

How does smoking marijuana help?

"I use it as prevention. I have not had my weekly headache since childhood. It has to be really good bud, and it relaxes me. It takes me to a higher spiritual place. It's part of my religious belief; it's a sacrament. Herbs and humans need each other. I'm a nature worshiper, and I can sanction anyone who uses Mother Nature's herb."

"Like most tearjerker myths, Peron's leaves a few things out. Such as the fact that he was a notorious San Francisco drug dealer for decades."

Pebbles introduces me to her friend Buzzy Linhart, a roly-poly, balding man with stiff whiskers the color of straw. Buzzy is wearing an eye patch. "If not for marijuana, Buzzy might well be blind," says Pebbles.

I ask Buzzy if I can see his doctor's note.

"I have to update my doctor's letter. I gotta go back to Berkeley and see if he's, uhhh, in the country."

Pebbles presses him, "Tell them about your disease."

At this point Buzzy launches into a dialogue I have great difficulty following: "I found my old pal marijuana saved my life . . . the love herb . . . gather the earth back together . . . Reagan . . . prostitution laws." Suddenly, he says, "This is important. Write this down," giving me hope I will get something useful. "Do you know who was the co-author of Bette Midler's 'Got to Have Friends'?"

Uh, no.

"Buzzy was the co-author. Tonight, she's opening in Las Vegas. People like her should not forget the people who launched their career."

Important Lessons

I make a mental note. Buzzy and Pebbles have taught me an important lesson. People who get high are very difficult to interview, for several reasons: (1) They can't complete a thought. They speak in strings of non-sequiturs; they dig for socially heavy meaning but can only come up with verbal scraps—snatches of movement jargon from the summer of love, stoner observations overheard in the parking lots at Dead shows, stray dialogue from "Gilligan's Island."

164

(2) They are paranoid. During our interview, Pebbles often strays out of the camera's range to stand very close to me and look at my notes. This is distracting because I do not want her to see, say, my description of her outfit. I resolve to write in very small letters. It is also distracting because it affords me an uncomfortably close view of her teeth, the kind of teeth I will see many more of in the days to come—brown and rotted with smoke, the color of dead flowers, and covered by a slimy film.

I decide to move on, determined to find out how the process works, how one gets a doctor to write a note and then procures a coveted membership card from the club. I move to the back room. Everyone here is smoking, although smoking is forbidden on the first floor, and none of them has a membership card yet. I sit down next to Lily White and Billy Swain, two friends who met at the club three years ago. Lily says she has eye problems and sciatica, a pain in her leg and thigh. I ask how she got her doctor's note: "I asked my doctor to prescribe marijuana. He didn't want to do it. But all he needs to know is that I need it. I'm the patient. The doctors should know it's our life, it's in our hands, not the doctor's hands. Why, are you thinking about becoming a patient?"

I tell her I have no serious problems.

"The majority of people are facing something, anxiety or depression," she comforts. "You know what problems you got. Even if you just want to hang out. You got to approach it as honest as you can. Do you like what you see, or don't you?" Billy Swain agrees: "It's not so much that you have to get your doctor's permission. They have to say yes to you. The doctors should cater to you. You have to figure out if you're bored, if you need a social outlet. This is a happy place; there's a lot of hugging." A burly ponytailed man named Fred Martin joins the group. "Can I have a toke?" he asks Lily, and a toke is offered. A former Hell's Angel, Martin lost the bottom half of his right leg in a motorcycle accident. Now he works as a professional activist, usually across the street from the White House, where he yells at President Bill Clinton as he jogs by, "Hey, I'll inhale for you." Fred offers his opinion on how I can join the club. "You women have a way of persuasion," he says, grinning, so I can admire his fine, mossy brown teeth. He picks up a pamphlet called *Medical Marijuana: Know Your Rights* put out by Peron, and reads it aloud: "'Talk with your doctor. Marijuana has been shown to: aid in stress management.' Don't you ever get stressed out?" he

> *"[Peron] seems to judge medical need haphazardly; his only guiding principle is deference to the patient."*

asks me. I look at him blankly, and he takes advantage of the silence to launch into the pot speech, something about Thomas Jefferson getting high, the Constitution on hemp paper, the War of 1812, Nancy Drew. . . .

At this point I had to stop. Total objectivity is a futile goal for all reporters, I realize. But there are times when personal circumstances so intrude on a reporter's judgment that they must be revealed. In this case, it could be that I have a boy-friend who drives me mad with his marijuana ravings, or that my uncle eased his cancer pains with marijuana, or that Dennis Peron is my best friend. As it happens, none of those things is true. What this reporter must admit is that at this point, I was very, very high. I had been sitting in this back room for quite some time and a cloud of smoke had risen level with my nose, giving me an acute case of contact high. I was not exactly hallucinating, but it seemed to me that everyone had stopped what they were doing and were staring at me. That Billy, Lily, Fred, even Van Gogh, were watching to see what I would do next. I decided it was time to go.

Not an Egomaniac?

The next morning I returned to meet Dennis Peron. His office is behind a bolted door with no door knob, in a corner of the building. Inside is the combi-nation of seedy and healthy living peculiar to California hippies—bits of weed and papers strewn about the stained carpet, alongside organic hemp meal and bottles of Arrowhead spring water. Dennis is like that, too, tanned but wrinkled, a wiry face and neatly combed white hair. I ask him why he started the club, and he begins, instantly, as if a switch had been thrown, to spin a heart-wrenching tale: "The club is a eulogy to my young lover Jonathan, who died of AIDS. We were lovers for seven years, and I miss him every day of my life. He died a very painful death. He had KS lesions all over his face, and we would go to a restaurant and people would move away from him. I always dreamed of a place Jonathan

> *"Some doctors are wary of marijuana's effects, but willing to defer to their patient's wishes."*

could go and smoke pot and meet people with AIDS and not feel such stigma. It started out as a eulogy and has turned into a mission of mercy for the most powerless and gentle members of society."

The story is completely rehearsed, emotionless. As he tells it, Peron flips through Post-it notes on his calendar, stops to shout to his coworkers to find out when his next radio interview is. It is only when I ask him who is responsible for Proposition 215 that I get his attention. "Me. You're looking at the guy. I am not an egomaniac, but it was my pain that changed the nation. My loss inspired me to do something for this country."

Like most tearjerker myths, Peron's leaves a few things out. Such as the fact that he was a notorious San Francisco drug dealer for decades before he started the club; he ran the Big Top supermarket, a one-stop drug emporium, and the Island Restaurant, which served pot upstairs and food downstairs, and was in and out of jail several times.

Later, when I tell Zimmerman about Peron's version of the story, he laughs for a good ten seconds before he explains Peron's role. "After two months it be-came clear that Dennis was going to fail miserably, that he wasn't keeping up with projections." They needed 800,000 signatures in five months to qualify the proposition, and Peron only had a few thousand. "By the time we were finished he had provided less than 10 percent of the signatures. There is no limit to that man's ego."

Judging Medical Need

Peron does seem to be driven by an egotist's perverse, almost pathological need to shock. He believes he is infallible. He believes, actually, that he is literally a saint. He says things with no regard to the consequences, or perhaps too much regard. The most famous example is a quote he gave to the *New York Times* in 1996, a quote that was folded into the opponents' commercials, and cost Zimmerman countless hours of damage control: "I believe all marijuana use is medical—except for kids," he said. I ask Peron now if he regrets that quote. He stands up and glares at me. "No way do I regret it," he shouts. "I believe 90 percent to 100 percent of marijuana use is medical."

Needless to say, this attitude makes Peron's medical judgments less than scientific. He seems to judge medical need haphazardly; his only guiding principle is deference to the patient. For example, drug czar Barry McCaffrey, in his hostile December 1996 press conference, held up a chart he attributed to an ally of Peron's listing the medical uses of marijuana, including such dubious ailments as writer's cramp, aphrodisiac and recovering lost memories. "Aphrodisiac, that's ridiculous," Peron says, recalling the list. "They are just so uptight they had to throw in some sexual thing." What about the lost memories? "That's all right with me. Some people have demons, and they have to chase them away."

Narcotics agents busted him in August 1996 precisely for this laxness; among other things, they sent in an undercover female agent with a diagnosis of a yeast infection, and Peron sold her marijuana. He still does not understand why that's a problem. "I said to her, 'I'm kind of embarrassed, this is a woman's thing, but maybe it helps the itching.' I'm not going to second guess a woman. I'd be putting down every woman in the world if I denied her medicine."

The Process

By the end of our talk, I have a better understanding of the process, although I'm not sure I have more faith in it. Peron is more careful than he used to be, more out of concern for narcs than for his patients. At his press conference, Mc-Caffrey threatened to prosecute doctors who recommend the drug. This threat has ironically provided Peron with an easy excuse. "Everybody's being tricky," Peron says. "It's a semantic game forced on us by the federal government." The club operators ask only the minimum level of cooperation from the doctors: they check that the doctor is registered with the state licensing board, call the doctor, identify the club and check that the letter of diagnosis is real. Only if the doctor voices an objection will they deny the patient a membership card. It's an excuse, but not a great one. The other clubs still require a signed recommendation from the doctor. They also check with the doctor every six months or so to see that the diagnosis is still valid. Once a patient has a membership card from Peron's club, he has it forever.

The doctors who cooperate fall into three main categories. (1) Serious illness doctors. In cases of AIDS, cancer, glaucoma and epilepsy, there is substantial anecdotal evidence, although no thorough scientific research, that marijuana helps. For AIDS patients, it stimulates appetite; for cancer, it eases nausea associated with chemotherapy; for glaucoma, it relieves eye pressure; and, for epilepsy, it helps prevent seizures. (2) True believers. There are a handful of doctors who believe in marijuana's capacity to ease a myriad of symptoms. Most do independent research and monitor their patients carefully. (3) The skeptical but convinceable. Here is where the practice gets fishy.

Some doctors are wary of marijuana's effects, but willing to defer to their patient's wishes. Ironically, Proposition 215 permits them to cede control over marijuana much more than they could over, say, allergy medicine. An allergy medicine prescription has to be signed and numbered and tracked, with the number of refills designated. Marijuana merely has to be approved, and an oral approval will do. Dr. Barry Zevin runs the Tom Waddell Clinic in San Francisco, serving the poor and underserved. He says hundreds of his patients have asked him for letters of diagnosis to use at Peron's club. In 10 percent of the cases, mostly AIDS and cancer, he hands them over confidently. In 10 percent he advises against it, such as when the patient is severely psychotic. And for the rest he is not sure. But he will never deny a patient, even a psychotic one, a letter of diagnosis, and he is not sure he would ever make clear his objections. Because of his uncertainty, Peron's laxness suits him: "I try to educate my patients. I say, 'The last thing in the world you need is marijuana. The last time you smoked it you became psychotic.' But if they still want a letter, it's a dilemma. . . . I prefer it to remain a gray area, where I don't need to make a decision." Even if Zevin persists in objecting, he may be won over. "Knowing them, they would have some advocacy," he says of the club operators. "They would call and say, 'Would you reconsider? We have some research that shows marijuana helps hangnails, and I think this person ought to get it.' It's a process of negotiation.". . .

> *"There is something a little bleak about the new pot atmosphere. . . . The puffing up of marijuana into something more than it is."*

A Sad Pretense

When all the buzz has faded, there is something a little bleak about the new pot atmosphere. Not that it might lead to legalization; that doesn't much bother me. But the air of sanctimony; the puffing up of marijuana into something more than it is. . . .

For the sick, this blithe reverence for the herb seems especially grim. I suppose if you are a terminal AIDS or cancer patient, smoking pot every once in a while, even every day, can't hurt much. But knowing, even with medical certainty, that THC stimulates the anandamide neurotransmitter says nothing about what it does to your general well being. Pot may be medicine, but getting high every day is still getting high every day. And it can't be good for Dennis Peron's depressed stragglers and veterans on SSI to sit around getting high every day.

Spend a few days hanging around Peron's club, and you can get awfully sad at the pretense that all the wretched souls—the sick and the sick at heart—can be fixed by a hug and a toke.

State Medical Marijuana Laws Should Be Opposed

by Joseph A. Califano Jr.

About the author: *Joseph A. Califano Jr. is the president of the National Center on Addiction and Substance Abuse at Columbia University.*

Surely the right to speak in support of any idea, however outrageous, carries the obligation not to lie about it. Despite the battery of television spots in which office-seekers splattered each other with negative ads, false accusations and slanderous innuendos, the Anything Goes Emmy for Political Hoodwink in 1996 does not go to a candidate. It belongs to the campaigns in Arizona and California to pass pro-drug legalization propositions, sold to voters as getting tough on violent criminals and offering compassionate care for the dying.

And the award for best supporting role goes to billionaire George Soros, the Daddy Warbucks of drug legalization. He doesn't reside in either state, but he bankrolled both efforts.

Bamboozling the Voters

What makes it critical for Americans to understand how Arizona and California voters were bamboozled is the announced intention of pro-legalization forces to take their misleading advertising campaigns state-by-state across America.

Arizona Prop. 200 makes it legal under state law for doctors to prescribe LSD, heroin and marijuana—drugs subject to the tightest federal controls because of dangers inherent in their use and the absence of medicinal value commensurate with those dangers. But of 10 ads promoting Prop. 200, not one mentioned that it loosened controls on LSD or heroin; only one noted—in passing for five seconds—that the proposal let doctors prescribe marijuana for seriously and terminally ill patients.

The Arizona ads trumpeted Prop. 200 as a law requiring violent criminals to serve their full sentences and supporting drug prevention and education. In a monument of chutzpa, one TV ad accused opponents of being "drug legalizers

Excerpted from "Devious Efforts to Legalize Drugs," by Joseph A. Califano Jr., *The Washington Post,* December 4, 1996. Reprinted with permission from the author.

and liquor lobbyists" fighting to preserve their profits from the 1,000 percent jump in drug use and 300 percent rise in alcohol use in Arizona elementary schools.

In California, TV ads dressed Prop. 215 in the drag of a law permitting doctors to give dying patients marijuana for their nausea from chemotherapy, increase the appetites of wasting cancer and AIDS victims, and relieve their pain. In fact, the proposition permits marijuana to be given to individuals of any age—including children—for any illness and without prescription, simply on the oral recommendation of any doctor.

The National Center on Addiction and Substance Abuse at Columbia University surveyed California voters two weeks before the election. Fifty-eight percent favored making marijuana available to terminally ill patients. (Not surprisingly, 56 percent of voters favored Prop. 215 on Election Day.) But most surveyed voters opposed making marijuana available for any illness, at any age and without a doctor's prescription, merely on a physician's verbal recommendation—three things that Prop. 215 does. Indeed, once respondents understood these provisions, most believed that Prop. 215 would increase teenage marijuana use and invite abuse from individuals using and selling pot for nonmedical purposes.

Out-of-State Money

Most money used to buy misleading TV ads for both referenda came from out of state. In Arizona, of $300,490 contributed to support Prop. 200, only $490 came from in state. The remaining $300,000 came from out of state, $200,000 of it from the Drug Policy Foundation—a pet charity of George Soros's—and the other $100,000 came directly from Soros himself.

Of the $1.8 million in reported contributions (as of Oct. 31, 1996) to support Prop. 215 in California, $1.4 million came from out of state. Here again, the biggest bucks—at least $550,000—came from Soros, who lives and amasses his wealth 3,000 miles away in New York City.

Private money always has held the power to corrupt governments, thwart the will of the majority and protect powerful interests by unduly influencing politicians. Politics is a wide-open arena where life is unfair and rules are as loose as those in an illegal cock fight. We're supposed to rely on the instincts of voters to sort it all out and come to sound conclusions.

> *"Proposition [215] permits marijuana to be given to individuals of any age— including children— for any illness and without prescription."*

But in California and Arizona, the voters never had a chance. A moneyed, out-of-state elite mounted a cynical and deceptive campaign to push its hidden agenda to legalize drugs. How do we establish accountability to tell the truth in such advertising? Surely some obligation, moral if not legal, to speak the truth goes along with the right to speak in support of any idea, however outrageous.

Opposition

Other states threatened with the same huckstering that duped Arizona and California voters should consider legislation to curb the use of out-of-state money. Congress might act to protect states from being turned into playpens for elites to try out their ideas where they don't have to live with (or pay taxes to deal with) the consequences.

> *"States . . . should consider legislation to curb the use of out-of-state money."*

Our children are at stake here. Individuals who make it through age 21 without using drugs, smoking or abusing alcohol are almost certain never to do so. Yet our record in keeping legal drugs out of the hands of children is pitiful: 5 million children smoke cigarettes, and millions more underage youngsters drink alcohol.

A state has an enormous interest in protecting children from proposals likely to make drugs such as marijuana, heroin and LSD more acceptable and accessible. It certainly is sufficient to require proponents of looser regulation to identify themselves and the sources of their money clearly and to describe their propositions accurately.

A parent's interest is even greater. Gen. Barry McCaffrey, the administration's "drug czar," said supporters of the campaigns in Arizona and California should be ashamed of themselves. But what about parents who didn't battle Props. 200 and 215? Parents who didn't even come out to vote? And what about parents in states Mr. Soros and his colleagues have targeted for their next pro-legalization drive if parents don't organize now to protect their children? Unlike parents in California and Arizona, they cannot claim ignorance as a defense.

Bibliography

Books

David Sadofsky Baggins	*Drug Hate and the Corruption of American Justice*. Westport, CT: Praeger, 1998.
Dan Baum	*Smoke and Mirrors: The War on Drugs and the Politics of Failure*. Boston: Little, Brown and Company, 1996.
William Bennett	*Body Count: Moral Poverty—and How to Win America's War Against Crime and Drugs*. New York: Simon & Schuster, 1996.
Eva Bertram et al.	*Drug War Politics: The Price of Denial*. Berkeley: University of California Press, 1996.
Lorenz Böllinger, ed.	*Cannabis Science: From Prohibition to Human Right*. New York: Peter Lang, 1997.
Vincent T. Bugliosi	*The Phoenix Solution: Getting Serious About Winning America's Drug War*. Beverly Hills, CA: Dove Books, 1996.
Jonathan P. Caulkins et al.	*Mandatory Minimum Drug Sentences: Throwing Away the Key or the Taxpayers' Money?* Santa Monica, CA: Rand, 1997.
Ron Chepesiuk	*Hard Target: The United States War Against International Drug Trafficking, 1982–1997*. Jefferson, NC: McFarland, 1999.
Dirk Chase Eldredge	*Ending the War on Drugs: A Solution for America*. Bridgehampton, NY: Bridge Works, 1998.
Jefferson M. Fish, ed.	*How to Legalize Drugs*. Northvale, NJ: Jason Aronson, 1998.
H. Richard Friman	*NarcoDiplomacy: Exporting the U.S. War on Drugs*. Ithaca, NY: Cornell University Press, 1996.
Mike Gray	*Drug Crazy: How We Got into This Mess and How We Can Get Out*. New York: Random House, 1998.
Lester Grinspoon and James B. Bakalar	*Marihuana, the Forbidden Medicine*. New Haven, CT: Yale University Press, 1997.
Institute of Medicine	*Marijuana and Medicine: Assessing the Science Base*. Washington, DC: National Academy Press, 1999.

Drug Legalization

Jill Jonnes	*Hep-Cats, Narcs, and Pipe Dreams: A History of America's Romance with Illegal Drugs*. New York: Scribner, 1996.
Robert L. Maginnis	*Legalization of Drugs: The Myths and the Facts*. Washington, DC: Family Research Council, 1995.
Michael Massing	*The Fix*. New York: Simon & Schuster, 1998.
Richard Lawrence Miller	*Drug Warriors and Their Prey: From Police Power to Police State*. Westport, CT: Praeger, 1996.
Craig Reinarman and Harry G. Levine, eds.	*Crack in America: Demon Drugs and Social Justice*. Berkeley: University of California Press, 1997.
Kevin Jack Riley	*Snow Job? The War Against International Cocaine Trafficking*. New Brunswick, NJ: Transaction, 1996.
Ed Rosenthal and Steve Kubby	*Why Marijuana Should Be Legal*. New York: Thunder's Mouth, 1996.
Jeffrey A. Schaler, ed.	*Drugs: Should We Legalize, Decriminalize, or Deregulate?* Amherst, NY: Prometheus, 1998.
Paul B. Stares	*Global Habit: The Drug Problem in a Borderless World*. Washington, DC: Brookings Institution, 1996.
Thomas Szasz	*Our Right to Drugs: The Case for a Free Market*. New York: Syracuse University Press, 1996.
William O. Walker III	*Drugs in the Western Hemisphere: An Odyssey of Cultures in Conflict*. Wilmington, DE: Scholarly Resources, 1996.

Periodicals

Eva Bertram and Kenneth Sharpe	"Escalation=More Drugs," *Nation*, March 29, 1999.
David D. Boaz	"Battling the Drug Demon," *USA Today*, May 1999.
Richard Brookhiser	"Lost in the Weed," *U.S. News & World Report*, January 13, 1997.
Willie Brown Jr.	"Don't Bar a Pain Killer OK'd by Voters," *Los Angeles Times*, April 8, 1998. Available from Reprints, Times Mirror Square, Los Angeles, CA 90053.
Joseph A. Califano Jr.	"Legalization of Narcotics: Myths and Reality," *USA Today*, March 1997.
Joseph A. Califano Jr.	"Marijuana: It's a Hard Drug," *Washington Post*, September 30, 1997. Available from 1150 15th St. NW, Washington, DC 20071.
Gina Chon	"Medical Marijuana: A Dream up in Smoke?" *Human Rights*, Fall 1997.
Thomas W. Clark	"Keep Marijuana Illegal—for Teens," *Humanist*, May/June 1997.
Thomas A. Constantine	"The War We're Not Fighting," *American Legion*, June 1998. Available from PO Box 1055, Indianapolis, IN 46206.

Bibliography

Cynthia Cotts	"Pot Shots," *Village Voice*, March 30, 1999.
Theodore Dalrymple	"Don't Legalize Drugs," *City Journal*, Spring 1997. Available from the Manhattan Institute, 52 Vanderbilt Ave., 2nd Floor, New York, NY 10017.
Robert Dreyfuss	"Another Victory for Medical Marijuana," *Rolling Stone*, May 13, 1999.
Richard Estrada	"Drug Treatment vs. Legalization," *San Diego Union-Tribune*, December 14, 1998. Available from PO Box 191, San Diego, CA 92119-4106.
David M. Fine	"Grassroots Medicine," *American Prospect*, September/October 1997.
Steve Forbes	"Don't Be Deceived by Pushers of Drug Legalization," *Human Events*, September 26, 1997. Available from 422 First St. SE, Washington, DC 20003.
Dave Fratello	"The Medical Marijuana Menace," *Reason*, March 1998.
Milton Friedman	"There's No Justice in the War on Drugs," *New York Times*, January 11, 1998.
Nick Gillespie	"Prescription: Drugs," *Reason*, February 1997.
Jennifer Gonnerman	"Justice for Junkies," *Village Voice*, June 3, 1997.
William Norman Grigg	"Battle Lines in the Drug War," *New American*, October 27, 1997. Available from PO Box 8040, Appleton, WI 54912.
Issues and Controversies On File	"Drug Legalization," March 8, 1996. Available from Facts On File News Services, 11 Penn Plaza, New York, NY 10001-2006.
James Kitfield	"Update on the Drug Wars," *National Journal*, July 3, 1999.
Mark A.R. Kleiman	"Drugs and Drug Policy: The Case for a Slow Fix," *Issues in Science and Technology*, Fall 1998.
Helga Kuhse and Peter Singer	"From the Editors," *Bioethics*, vol. 11, no. 2, 1997. Available from 350 Main St., Malden, MA 02148.
Paul Leithart	"Marijuana as Medicine," *New American*, October 13, 1997.
Anthony Lewis	"The Noble Experiment," *New York Times*, January 5, 1998.
Barry R. McCaffrey	"Don't Legalize Those Drugs," *Washington Post*, June 29, 1999.
Barry R. McCaffrey	"Legalization Would Be the Wrong Direction," *Los Angeles Times*, July 27, 1998.
Ethan A. Nadelmann	"Commonsense Drug Policy," *Foreign Affairs*, January/February 1998.
Gabriel G. Nahas et al.	"Marijuana Is the Wrong Medicine," *Wall Street Journal*, March 11, 1997.
National Review	"War on Drugs Is Lost," special section, February 12, 1996.

175

Drug Legalization

Andrew O'Hehir	"Smoke and Mirrors: Clinton and His Drug Czar Defy the Voters on Medical Marijuana," *Spin*, April 1997. Available from PO Box 51513, Boulder, CO 80323-1513.
Dan Quayle	"Drug Legalizers Won Two Important, but Medically Outrageous, Victories," *Human Events*, December 13, 1996.
Charles B. Rangel	"Why Drug Legalization Should Be Opposed," *Criminal Justice Ethics*, June 22, 1998. Available from 899 Tenth Ave., New York, NY 10019-1029.
John S. Robey	"The Deconstitutionalized Zone," *Liberty*, March 1999.
A.M. Rosenthal	"Pointing the Finger," *New York Times*, June 12, 1998.
Sally Satel	"Do Drug Courts Really Work?" *City Journal*, Summer 1998.
Sally Satel	"Opiates for the Masses," *Wall Street Journal*, June 8, 1998.
Robert Scheer	"A Drug War Fought on Ideology Alone," *Los Angeles Times*, March 23, 1999.
Eric Schlosser	"More Reefer Madness," *Atlantic Monthly*, April 1997.
Joshua Wolf Shenk	"America's Altered States," *Harper's Magazine*, May 1999.
George Soros	"The Drug War 'Cannot Be Won': It's Time to Just Say No to Self-Destructive Prohibition," *Washington Post*, February 2, 1997.
Paul B. Stares	"Drug Legalization: Time for a Real Debate," *Brookings Review*, Spring 1996.
Rob Stewart	"Principles of Reform," *Drug Policy Letter*, January/February 1998. Available from 4455 Connecticut Ave. NW, Suite B-500, Washington, DC 20008-2302.
Mark Steyn	"Call Off the Drug War," *American Spectator*, April 1999.
Mortimer B. Zuckerman	"Great Idea for Ruining Kids," *U.S. News & World Report*, February 24, 1997.

Organizations to Contact

The editors have compiled the following list of organizations concerned with the issues debated in this book. The descriptions are derived from materials provided by the organizations. All have publications or information available for interested readers. The list was compiled on the date of publication of the present volume; the information provided here may change. Be aware that many organizations take several weeks or longer to respond to inquiries, so allow as much time as possible.

Canadian Centre on Substance Abuse (CCSA)
75 Albert St., Suite 300, Ottawa, ON K1P 5E7, CANADA
(613) 235-4048 • fax: (613) 235-8101
e-mail: info@ccsa.ca • website: http://www.ccsa.ca

Established in 1988 by an act of Parliament, the CCSA works to minimize the harm associated with the use of alcohol, tobacco, and other drugs. It disseminates information on the nature, extent, and consequences of substance abuse; sponsors public debate on the topic; and supports organizations involved in substance abuse treatment, prevention, and educational programming. The center publishes the newsletter *Action News* six times a year.

Canadian Foundation for Drug Policy (CFDP)
70 MacDonald St., Ottawa, ON K2P 1H6, CANADA
(613) 236-1027 • fax: (613) 238-2891
e-mail: eoscapel@fox.nstn.ca • website: http://www.cfdp.ca

Founded by several of Canada's leading drug policy specialists, CFDP examines the objectives and consequences of Canada's drug laws and policies. When necessary, the foundation recommends alternatives that it believes would be more effective and humane. CFDP disseminates educational materials and maintains a website.

Cato Institute
1000 Massachusetts Ave. NW, Washington, DC 20001-5403
(202) 842-0200 • fax: (202) 842-3490
e-mail: cato@cato.org • website: http://www.cato.org

The institute, a libertarian public policy research foundation dedicated to limiting the control of government and protecting individual liberty, strongly favors drug legalization. Its publications include on-line commentaries, policy analyses, the *Cato Journal*, published three times a year, and the bimonthly *Cato Policy Report*.

Drug Enforcement Administration (DEA)
700 Army-Navy Dr., Arlington, VA 22202
(202) 307-1000
website: http://www.usdoj.gov/dea

The DEA is the division of the federal Department of Justice that is charged with enforcing the nation's drug laws. The agency concentrates on stopping the smuggling and distribution of narcotics in the United States and abroad. Its website contains data on drug use and arrest rates as well as fact sheets, intelligence reports, and the books *Drugs of Abuse*, *Get It Straight: The Facts About Drugs*, and *Speaking Out Against Drug Legalization*.

Drug Policy Foundation

4455 Connecticut Ave. NW, Suite B-500, Washington, DC 20008-2328
(202) 537-5005 • fax: (202) 537-3007
e-mail: dpf@dpf.org • website: http://www.dpf.org

The foundation is a nonprofit organization that opposes the war on drugs and supports a variety of drug policy reform approaches, including decriminalization, legalization, medicalization, and harm reduction. Its publications include the bimonthly *Drug Policy Letter* and the book *The Great Drug War*. It also distributes *Press Clips*, an annual compilation of newspaper articles on drug legalization issues, as well as legislative updates.

The Heritage Foundation

214 Massachusetts Ave. NE, Washington, DC 20002-4999
(202) 546-4400 • fax (202) 546-8328
e-mail: info@heritage.org • website: http://www.heritage.org

The Heritage Foundation is a conservative public policy research institute that opposes drug legalization and advocates strengthening law enforcement to stop drug abuse. It publishes policy analyses on a broad range of topics, including drug issues. Its regular publications include the monthly *Policy Review*, the Backgrounder series of occasional papers, and the Heritage Lecture series.

Libertarian Party

2600 Virginia Ave. NW, Suite 100, Washington, DC 20037
(202) 333-0008 • fax: (202) 333-0072
e-mail: hq@lp.org • website: http://www.lp.org

The Libertarian Party is a political party that seeks limited government and promotes individual liberty. It advocates the repeal of all laws prohibiting the production, sale, possession, or use of drugs. The party believes law enforcement should focus on preventing violent crimes against persons and property rather than on prosecuting people who use drugs. It publishes the monthly *Libertarian Party News* as well as fact sheets, books, and brochures including *Towards a More Sensible Drug Policy*.

Lindesmith Center

400 W. 59th St., New York, NY 10019
(212) 548-0695 • fax: (212) 548-4670
e-mail: esherifova@sorosny.org • website: http://www.lindesmith.org

The Lindesmith Center is a policy research institute that focuses on broadening the debate on drug policy and related issues. The center is critical of current prohibitionist drug policies and favors policies based on harm reduction. Particular attention is focused on analyzing the experiences of foreign countries that have liberalized their drug laws. The center publishes research briefs and books, including *Marijuana Myths, Marijuana Facts: A Review of the Scientific Evidence*. It also makes available the full text of many journal articles, reports, and other materials on its website.

Media Awareness Project (MAP)

PO Box 651, Porterville, CA 93258
(800) 266-5759
e-mail: mgreer@mapinc.org • website: http://mapinc.org

MAP is an international network of activists dedicated to drug policy reform, with an emphasis on impacting public opinion and media coverage of drug policy issues. It opposes the criminal justice/prosecution/interdiction model of drug policy and favors a more liberal approach. MAP publishes the weekly *DrugSense* newsletter and makes tens of thousands of drug policy–related articles available on its website.

National Center on Addiction and Substance Abuse at Columbia University (CASA)
152 W. 57th St., 12th Floor, New York, NY 10019-3310
(212) 841-5200 • fax: (212) 956-8020
website: http://www.casacolumbia.org

CASA is a private, nonprofit organization that works to educate the public about the hazards of chemical dependency. The organization opposes drug legalization and supports treatment as the best way to reduce drug addiction. It produces publications describing the harmful effects of alcohol and drug addiction and effective ways to address the problem of substance abuse. It also distributes the monthly newsletter *Start* and makes reports and articles available on its website.

National Institute on Drug Abuse (NIDA)
6001 Executive Blvd., Bethesda, MD 20892
website: http://www.nida.nih.gov

NIDA is a division of the National Institutes of Health in the U.S. Department of Health and Human Services. It supports and conducts research on drug abuse—including the yearly Monitoring the Future Survey—to improve addiction prevention, treatment, and policy efforts. It publishes fact sheets, reports, the bimonthly *NIDA Notes* newsletter, and pamphlets such as *Marijuana: Facts for Teens*.

National Organization for the Reform of Marijuana Laws (NORML)
1001 Connecticut Ave. NW, Suite 710, Washington, DC 20036
(202) 483-5500 • fax: (202) 483-0057
e-mail: norml@norml.org • website: http://www.norml.org

NORML fights to legalize marijuana and to help those who have been convicted and sentenced for possessing or selling marijuana. It publishes an on-line newsletter, reports, and books including *Marihuana: The Forbidden Medicine* and *Marijuana Myths, Marijuana Facts*.

Office of National Drug Control Policy (ONDCP)
Drug Policy Information Clearinghouse
PO Box 6000, Rockville, MD 20849-6000
(800) 666-3332 • fax: (301) 519-5212
e-mail: ondcp@ncjrs.org/
website: http://www.whitehousedrugpolicy.gov

The ONDCP is the White House office responsible for formulating the government's national drug strategy and the president's antidrug policy as well as coordinating the federal agencies responsible for stopping drug trafficking. It publishes the annual *National Drug Control Strategy* and offers a wide variety of fact sheets, reports, and other publications on its website.

RAND Corporation
1700 Main St., PO Box 2138, Santa Monica, CA 90407-2138
(310) 393-0411 • fax: (310) 393-4818
e-mail: correspondence@rand.org • website: http://www.rand.org

The RAND Corporation is a research institution that seeks to improve public policy through research and analysis. RAND's Drug Policy Research Center publishes information on the costs, prevention, and treatment of drug abuse as well as on trends in drug-law enforcement. It publishes reports, research briefs, and books, including *An*

Ounce of Prevention, a Pound of Uncertainty: The Cost-Effectiveness of School-Based Drug Prevention Programs and *Mandatory Minimum Drug Sentences: Throwing Away the Key or the Taxpayers' Money?*

Reason Foundation
3415 S. Sepulveda Blvd., Suite 400, Los Angeles, CA 90034
(310) 391-2245 • fax: (310) 391-4395
e-mail: gpassantino@reason.org • website: http://www.reason.org

Reason is a libertarian public policy research foundation dedicated to limited government and individual freedom. It opposes America's war on drugs and strongly favors drug legalization. It publishes books and booklets, including *Reason Drug Reader*, policy studies, and the monthly magazine *Reason*, which periodically contains articles on drug policy issues.

Index

ad campaigns
  are ineffective, 18
AIDS, 106
  needle exchange programs to combat,
    78, 82–83, 97, 106
  as secondary effect of drugs, 77
  wasting syndrome, 132
    cannabis used in treatment of,
      145–46, 147
Ain't Nobody's Business If You Do: The
  Absurdity of Consensual Crimes in Our
  Free Country (McWilliams), 50
alcohol, 72, 75, 96
  consumption, effects of Prohibition on,
    85–86
  implication in traffic fatalities, 115
American Civil Liberties Union (ACLU),
  13, 133
American Journal of Public Health, 114
American Society of Clinical Oncology,
  144
Arciniega, Albert, 62, 63
arrests, drug, 42
  for marijuana, 133, 139, 151
Ashcroft, John, 18

Bachus, Spencer, 66
Barr, Bob, 151
Bedoya, Harold, 33
Belaunde, Fernando, 63
Bennett, William J., 57, 70, 132
Bertram, Eva, 81
Boaz, David D., 12, 41
Britain
  heroin maintenance in, 128–29
Buckley, William F., Jr., 43, 52, 101, 110
Bush, George, 57, 106

Califano, Joseph A., Jr., 14, 153, 170
cancer
  cannabis used in treatment of, 143–44,
    168

cannabis. *See* marijuana
Carbajal, Julio, 62
cartels, drug, 66
Carter administration, 102
Chain, Ernst, 142
civil liberties
  and marijuana prohibition, 134–35
  threat of drug laws on, 45, 49–55,
    86–87
Clinton, Bill, 17, 33, 39, 72, 106, 139
Clinton administration
  position on medical marijuana, 81, 134
cocaine
  crack, 56, 95
  decline in use of, 95
  implication in traffic fatalities, 114
  interdiction of, 27, 28, 65
  reasons behind use of, 99–100
  reduction in use of, 31
  sources of, 66
  supplies of, 42
Collins, Larry, 118
Colombia
  narcoguerrilla organizations in, 35
Constantine, Thomas A., 51, 66, 121
costs
  of drug law enforcement, 41–42, 44,
    106
  societal
    DEA estimation of legalization
      effects, 26
    of drug abuse, 30–31
crime
  drug-induced, 25–26
    vs. drug prohibition–related crime,
      91–92
  is driven by addiction, 117
  liberalizing drug policies would reduce,
    89–94
  as secondary effect of drugs, 77
  violent
    aggressive law enforcement has